Quilt Mavens

Perfect Paper Piecing

DEB KARASIK•
•JANET MEDNICK

American Quilter's Society

P. O. Box 3290 • Paducah, KY 42002-3290
www.AmericanQuilter.com

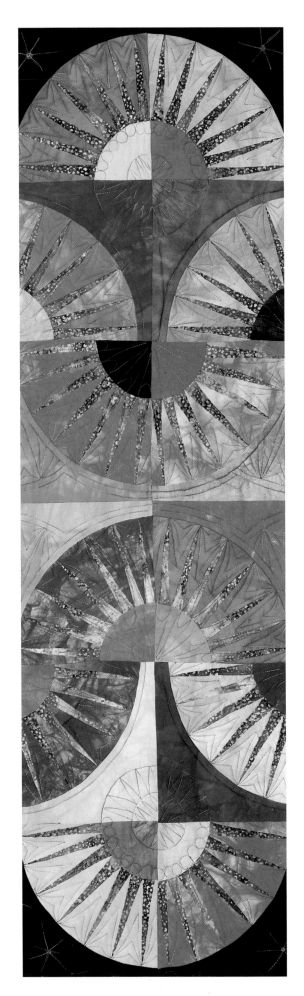

Located in Paducah, Kentucky, the American Quilter's Society (AQS) is dedicated to promoting the accomplishments of today's quilters. Through its publications and events, AQS strives to honor today's quiltmakers and their work and to inspire future creativity and innovation in quiltmaking.

EDITOR: BARBARA SMITH
GRAPHIC DESIGN: ELAINE WILSON
COVER DESIGN: MICHAEL BUCKINGHAM
QUILT PHOTOGRAPHY: CHARLES R. LYNCH
HOW-TO PHOTOGRAPHY: JEFFREY KARASIK

Library of Congress Cataloging-in-Publication Data

Karasik, Deb.
   Quiltmavens: perfect paper piecing / by Deb Karasik and Janet Mednick.
p. cm.
   Summary: "Learn how to make sharp spikes the QuiltMavens way by flipping, folding, and trimming your fabric--a new method for foundation paper piecing your quilts. Accuracy of points and curves are guaranteed. The accompanying CD contains all the patterns at full-size so you can print without copy machine distortion"--Provided by publisher.
   ISBN 978-1-57432-919-3
   1. Patchwork--Patterns. 2. Machine quilting--Patterns. I. Mednick, Janet. II. Title.

TT835.K378 2007
746.46'041--dc22

                        2006037350

Additional copies of this book may be ordered from the American Quilter's Society, PO Box 3290, Paducah, KY 42002-3290; 800-626-5420 (orders only please); or online at www.AmericanQuilter.com. For all other inquiries, call 270-898-7903.

Dedication

I lovingly dedicate this book to the memory of my mother, Hannah (Ann) Kantrowitz, an avid needlewoman and knitter extraordinaire, from whom I definitely inherited my love of fiber and cloth. Though money might have been in short supply when I was a child, she always found enough for yarn, fabric, beads, or paints. I can still hear her saying, "You can never be lonely if you have a hobby," her stock response anytime anyone, adult or child, whined that they were bored or had nothing to do. Another of her mottoes was "Never make any pattern or kit exactly as shown or written. Change something. Make it your own." If I was knitting a sweater, she taught and expected me to change a ribbed cuff to cables or add side slits at the hem. Needlepoint canvases were to be worked in various stitches and colors other than those painted in. I grew up thinking that everyone did this. That everyone could do this. I grew up knowing that I could! Thank you, Mom.

Thanks, too, to my husband, Avram, for thirty plus years of giving me room (literally and spiritually) for all my creative endeavors.

Janet Mednick

I'd like to dedicate this book to several people who have been key in my life: first of all, my amazing husband, Jeff, who has kept me laughing for thirty-three years. He has continually encouraged me to follow my dreams and embrace my passion for this wonderful textile art. I would also like to dedicate it to my two beautiful daughters, Sarah and Lauren, who continue to encourage me and graciously accept the quilts I make; and last but not least, to Debbie and Sue Deal, the original "spikettes," who originally encouraged me to write this book.

Deb Karasik

Acknowledgments

*W*e would like to thank the following folks for their amazing support. All of the following companies have continued to make this wonderful quilting journey a reality for us both. Deb & Janet

Babylock Sewing Machines

Hobbs Bonded Fibers

Hoffman California Fabrics

Janome Sewing Machines

Superior Threads

Contents

Introduction

The two of us began quilting at different times, different places, and for different reasons. And, like most quilters, the reasons we keep making quilts have changed over time. Some quilts are made as objects of beauty and considered works of art. Other quilts are made to be useful coverings. They can be playful or serious, a warming comfort, or an expression of love for family and friends. Many quilts represent various combinations of the above and more.

The designing and making of quilts allow us, as quiltmakers, to express our creative energies, making artists of everyday people. Quilts can be made by hand with the most basic sewing tools or on expensive sewing machines in fully equipped sewing studios. Whether you are young or old, a beginner or a master stitcher, a beautiful quilt of some sort is an achievable goal and a satisfying accomplishment. Best of all, it's fun!

Deb continues: When we became friends a few short years ago, we had a lot in common, both personally and as stitchers, but we were still in very different places quiltwise. I was relatively new to quilting, loved to paper piece and to hand dye much of my fabric, and I was already in love with spikes, as in the New York Beauty. Janet's style was to alter traditional patterns and then tweak them with unexpected choices of printed fabrics in bold colors, paper piecing only when absolutely necessary. She never found a method of paper piecing that didn't seem wasteful, time consuming, and tediously clumsy. Once I showed Janet my method, she learned that paper piecing could be quick, efficient, and actually fun. Who knew?

I rapidly became influenced by the way Janet successfully used prints, so I started working print fabrics into my own pieces. On the other hand, Janet was impressed by what I could create on my computer. She would throw out design ideas, and I would create them in moments with my computer. It quickly became a creative process we both enjoyed, and the ideas never seem to diminish.

Janet has always quilted her own work on her home machine, while I "knew" I would never be able to quilt like that. However, with Janet's persistent encouragement, I finally tried and found that it was much easier and more fun than I had anticipated. Now I quilt all my own work, and on collaborative pieces, I share the quilting with Janet.

Janet continues: As the months went by, we found we had another great bond in common. Neither of us was inspired by any of the quilt patterns we were seeing in magazines and books. They seemed to be repetitive, simply old quilts with new fabrics and new names. We wanted to make a quilt together, a project that not only challenged us but was exciting and fun to work on. Of course, it had to have spikes, and it had to be different from anything we'd ever seen. We bounced ideas back and forth and used the computer to design some quilts that really excited us. SPIKE REDUX was the first of many.

Janet and Deb continue: Our fellow quilters were supportive, to say the least. They oohed and aahed over our work at guild meetings. They encouraged us to keep designing, and they wanted to buy all of our patterns, which we were far from ready to produce, let alone sell. They wanted lessons, help with fabric choices, and quilting advice. The classes we taught were always full, with waiting lists. Meanwhile, our quilts were beginning to win a number of ribbons, and we were getting congratulations from complete strangers.

While attending Art Quilt Tahoe in 2004, we used after-hour class time to assemble ILLUMINATA. Other students were impressed and encouraged us to keep designing. What has continually impressed us the most, however, is the enthusiasm that our work has generated in others. Quilters want to keep learning and stretching their skills, both technically and creatively. They are open to trying something new and exploring new ideas. Our hope is to fill that niche, to inspire quilters of different experience levels to try something new. Maybe the pattern or the sewing technique will be that something. Maybe working outside one's color comfort zone or perhaps machine quilting for the first time will be the challenge. Let your imagination soar and start that new quilt! Oh…and we'd love to see it when it's done!

chapter 1

The *Basics*

Color and Cloth

When choosing fabrics, not only do we have to decide what colors to work with, we also have to create pleasing color combinations and arrange these colors in the quilt's overall design. Sounds like a lot to do before you even get started sewing, doesn't it?

But wait … we aren't done yet. Even if we know what colors we want to use, we still have to wade through the hundreds of enticing printed fabrics that exist these days in every color possible. There are tone-on-tone prints, batiks, paisleys, stripes, dots—you name it. And then there are multicolor prints. It's amazing that we get quilts made at all, don't you think? It's no wonder that so many quilters see a quilt they like in a book or magazine and duplicate it as closely as possible, not only matching colors but searching everywhere for the exact same fabric prints used in the original. After all, they see it, they like it, so they know the finished product will be successful.

It's flattering when other quilters and students copy our color choices, but we think they are missing out on the fun and personal gratification of making their own fabric choices. We make quilts in colors that please us, that make us happy, that seem right to us as we are designing and sewing, and we sometimes choose prints that even make us laugh. (Actually, that's more of a Janet thing than a Deb thing). To us it's all part of the big picture and the process of making a quilt or wallhanging.

Neither of us attended art school, nor have we taken any formal color theory classes, so we are not about to lecture on the subject. We base our color and fabric decisions on the experience and the information we've gained by making quilts and clothing over the years. Each quilt teaches us something new about how the big three of color, value, and intensity intermingle to produce a good quilt (and sometimes a not so good quilt … oh well).

So, here are some QuiltMaven™ color ideas to get you started or help you along when picking fabrics on your own.

Start with your favorite color. What is your favorite color? A simple question for some—not so simple for others. We have found that many people in our classes can't answer this question. At first, we were admittedly a little stunned by the blank faces, but it occurred again and again. If you are one of these people, not to worry, there's hope!

When you go fabric shopping, if the bolts are arranged by color, what section are you drawn to? What color makes you linger, reaching out to draw your hand along the shelves? Is it red? Orange? Lime green? That may be your favorite color.

Don't be afraid to try something new. Some of our best quilts were created when we stepped out of our color comfort zone. We often find that it creates learning opportunities for us. It makes us really look at and analyze our color and fabric combinations. Working with colors that are outside your usual comfort zone will expand your intuitive knowledge of color theory and design.

Contrast brings life to the patterns. For some of us, it's easier to find fabrics that go well together but have very little contrast. Although matching fabrics to a main focal print has worked in the past, it may not allow the ideal contrast you need for spiky quilts. Lay your fabrics out and see if you can see a crisp, clean line where they meet. If not, well, try again. This is a good time to cut out some really crude spiky shapes and

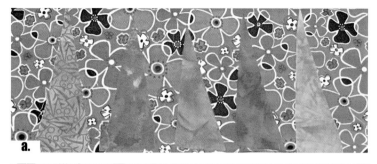

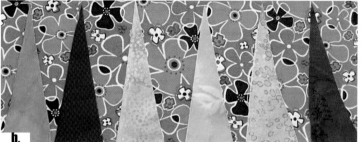

Fig. 1. Contrast: (a) These fabrics go with the background but don't provide any contrast. (b) These spikes can be easily seen against the background.

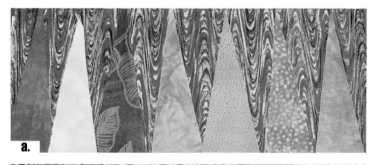

Fig. 2. Print scale: (a) Some of the spikes' edges get lost in the background. (b) Even though this background is busy, the spikes still show well.

lay them against your background to see if these smaller pieces still maintain their impact (fig. 1). Be careful what you choose for your spikes. It's easy to want to choose one of the colors from the focal fabric, but that choice might give you a spike that blends into the background.

Consider the scale of the print. The use of prints can make or break any quilt, but they are especially important when working with spikes. A bold print may work in a background, but using it in a spike will often cause the pattern to disappear and the spike to simply blend in (fig. 2). When you take the time to make paper-pieced spikes, you want those spikes to stand out.

"I'm much more comfortable using tone-on-tone fabrics, especially hand dyes and batiks without patterns. Janet hardly ever uses them. Her quilts are always a creative milkshake of all different patterns. She's got me working more and more with patterns now, and I have her filling in with tone-on-tone fabrics and hand dyes. I'm always surprised and delighted at the results!" Deb

Don't be afraid of making mistakes. How do you expect to learn if you never make mistakes? We all make them, and contrary to popular belief, it's not the end of the world. What we initially think of as mistakes can actually make some of our quilts more intriguing. You can always stop after a block or two and select a new fabric choice. If you're making one of our scrappier quilts and you're not quite happy with the way a particular fabric combination is working, keep on going. You can always use the block on the back.

"Although I'm as perfect as they come (not), I find that analyzing the mistakes I've made is the best way to learn something. I rarely make the same faux pas twice." Deb

Let your creativity fly! Making quilts in the same colors and fabrics that we have chosen is extremely flattering, but it would please us more if you worked with fabrics and colors that please you. If you love the reproduction fabrics of the 1860s, 1930s, or 1960s, by all means apply them to any of these projects.

Use subtle gradations of color. They add interest and can change the look of your creation. Gradations can be applied to the spikes, the background, the setting blocks, and the borders. As you can see in the example, color gradations can make a simple New York Beauty block into something extraordinary (fig. 3).

Paper-Piecing Method

Are you ready to start on the most exciting journey of your quilting career? Pull a comfy chair up to your sewing machine and let's get started.

Although each of our patterns has its own set of idiosyncrasies, which will be addressed as we go, you'll find that the following guidelines for paper piecing spikes will make the process faster than you thought possible, and easier and more fun than you imagined.

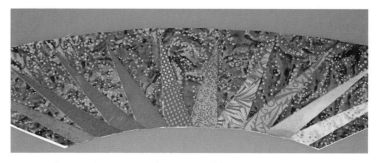

Fig. 3. Color gradations can bring new life to your quilts.

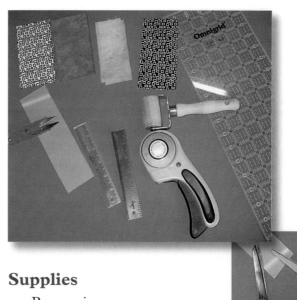

Supplies

Paper scissors
Fabric scissors
Small thread clipper
Rotary cutter and mat
Rotary ruler
Hard edge tool
Iron or pressing tool
Template plastic
Glue stick
Marking pencil
And of course, fabric!

Using the CD

All of the patterns are given on the enclosed CD as PDF files, which can be viewed in Preview or Acrobat. The link to download Acrobat is included on the CD. The pattern CD included with your book makes it possible to print all the patterns from your computer's printer in the correct size, thus eliminating the trouble of copying and enlarging them from the pages of the book. The CD is easy to use and features a pdf-based program that runs from Adobe Reader 5.0 or higher. If you don't already have this program on your computer, it is a free download from Adobe.com, or you can copy it from this CD.

If the patterns don't automatically open when you load your CD, open the file <patternthumbnails.pdf>. From this page, you should be able to open any pattern by clicking on its thumbnail, or by clicking on its line on the contents page. If larger than 8½" x 11", the pattern will open in a separate multi-page document from which you can print the tiled pages for easy assembly. Control+P will open your print dialogue box, or you can click on the <print pattern> link. Make sure you indicate which page numbers you want to print before sending the file to the printer.

Preparing Foundations

All of the patterns are mirror images of the blocks in the quilts. With foundation piecing, in which the fabrics are placed on the unmarked side of the pattern and sewn on the marked side, the finished blocks will end up looking like the ones in the quilts. For those parts of the blocks that are not foundation pieced, remember to place the templates on the wrong sides of the fabrics so they too will end up facing the right way.

From the CD, print copies of the block patterns to use as foundations. You will need a paper foundation for each block in your project.

Each block consists of at least three sections: a spiky unit, an inner arc, and an outer arc, regardless of the shape of the block. Cut the block sections apart. It's best to cut approximately ¼" outside the printed cutting line. You will trim to this line after sewing. Stack the sections in separate piles.

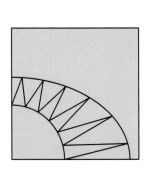
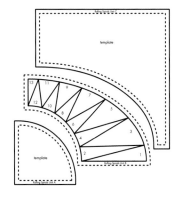
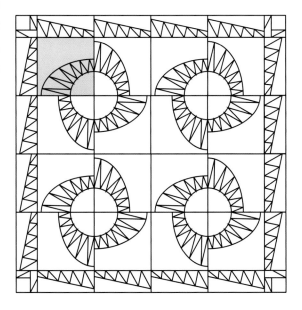

Precutting Fabrics

In a skewed arc, the spikes progressively change in size from one end of the arc to the other. In the cutting instructions for our patterns, we have given one size of fabric piece for all the spikes, based on the size of the largest one. Therefore, some of the fabric pieces will be quite large for the smallest spikes. The advantage of these large pieces is that they are easy to handle, and the trimmed away piece could be used again somewhere else.

If you prefer to save fabric, you can use the following measuring method to precut two sizes of fabric pieces, one for all the larger spikes and one for the smaller ones:

Place a rotary ruler over the spike (piece 2 in figure 4) so that the edge of the ruler aligns with the longest edge of the spike. Measure the length of the spike, and then, without moving the ruler, measure across the spike in a line perpendicular to the longest edge. Add about 1" to both measurements.

Example: The spike in figure 4 measures approximately 7/8" x 4". Round up to 1" x 4" and add 1" to both dimensions. Your precut fabric piece would then be 2" x 5". You can use this same measurement for spike pieces 4 and 6 in this arc.

For the remaining spikes, the fabric pieces can be shorter. Spike piece 8 is approximately 7/8" x 2 7/8" (fig. 5). Round up to 1" x 3" and add 1" to both measurements, which equals 2" x 4". Use these measurements to precut fabric pieces for spikes 10 and 12 also.

Measure and precut the fabric pieces for the background triangles in the same

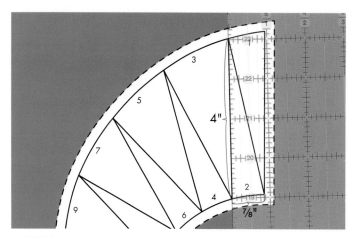

Fig. 4. Measuring a spike

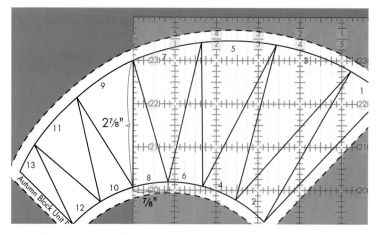

Fig. 5. Measuring smaller spikes

way. See the last tiny background piece in the figures? Although it is small, it will require a fabric scrap that extends to the cutting lines on all sides.

There are other shapes besides the skewed arc. In a regular arc (quarter circle), all the spikes are the same size, and all the background pieces are the same size. This makes cutting easy. Just multiply the number of spikes in an arc by the number of arcs needed to get the total number of fabric pieces needed. Repeat for the background pieces.

In blocks that are stretched into diamond shapes, the spikes change shape and size as they approach the center of the diamond. You could precut a different size fabric piece for each spike if you are trying to make a small amount of fabric go further or if each spike is to be cut from a different fabric.

"Although you're probably anxious to jump in and start sewing, being well prepared will make the process go much more smoothly. When I made my first quilt, I was extremely anxious to get it finished so I just started sewing, cutting fabric as I went. I made the entire quilt and started on the border before I realized this was a really silly approach. So I took the time to precut all the fabric for the border. The sewing went so fast, I was in awe. Okay, okay ... some of us are late learners or just really stubborn. I prefer to think of myself as just experimenting, trying all the techniques to see what works best." Deb

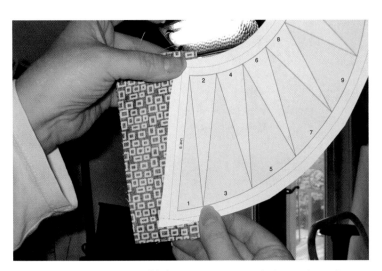

Fig. 6. Hold the pieces up to a light to place them.

Sewing Spikes

You're almost ready to sew! Make sure your machine needle is sharp. It's always a good idea to start with a new needle for each project, because paper will dull the needle quickly.

Set your stitch length at 1.0 or 1.5 (about 15 stitches per inch). Why so small? Well, as our students have learned, the smaller the stitch, the easier it is to remove the paper. This is especially important for the more extreme spiky units. Struggling with getting the paper off can stretch your fabric and pull the stitches. Neither of which is desirable.

1. Take precut pieces of background fabric and spike fabric and place them right sides together.

2. Place the fabric pieces underneath the pattern with the *wrong* side of the background fabric against the *unprinted* side of the pattern.

3. Hold the pattern up to a light source to make sure the fabrics cover the first background piece plus a seam allowance all around it (fig. 6). You can place a pin at both ends of the first seam line, if desired.

4. Lay the pattern on the sewing machine and sew on the line between pieces 1 and 2. It's desirable to sew from cutting line to cutting line, which will add stability.

5. Take the pattern off the sewing machine, turn it over, and press so that the first spike is covered by fabric (fig. 7, page 15).

"I use a two-dollar wallpaper roller to press open my seam allowances. They work great, and you don't need to plug them in." Deb

6. Turn the pattern print side up and align the hard-edge tool *along the next sewing line,* as shown in figure 8.

7. Fold the paper pattern back over the hard edge tool. Align the ¼" line of your ruler along this fold and use your rotary cutter to trim away the excess fabric, leaving the ¼" seam allowance (fig. 9).

8. Turn the pattern over and align the next background piece along the cut edge of the spike fabric, right sides together. Holding the fabric in place, carefully turn the foundation over and sew on the line for the second seam.

9. Repeat these steps until the template is completely covered with fabric. Turn the block to the paper side and trim

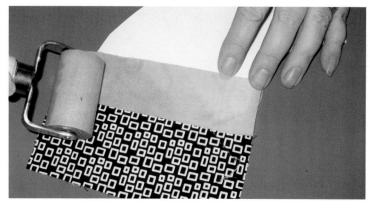

Fig. 7. Press the fabric over the spike.

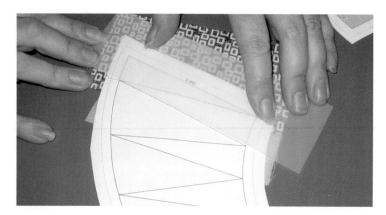

Fig. 8. Align the hard edge tool with the next seam line.

the foundation and the fabric on the dashed cutting line, but do not remove the paper yet (fig 10, page 16).

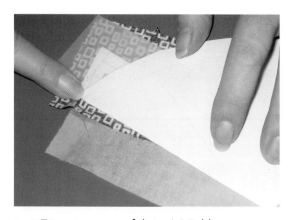

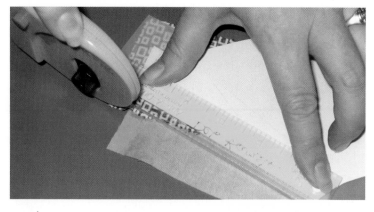

Fig. 9. Trimming excess fabric: (a) Fold paper pattern over tool.
(b) Measure a ¼" seam allowance and trim.

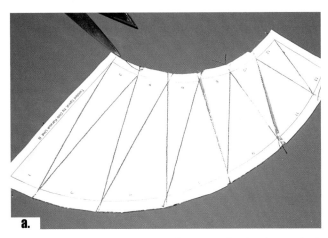

Fig. 10. Finished unit: (a) back of unit, (b) front of a unit sewn with different background fabric

Fig. 11. Marking centers: (a) Fold the pieces in half. (b) Mark the centers with pins.

"Have you noticed that you only have to hold the pattern up to the light once, don't have long clumsy fabric strips hanging in your way, and don't have to use pins? These are the features of this method that totally won me over to the fun of paper-piecing." Janet

Sewing Arcs

Great! You're done with your spiky units and ready to move on to complete the blocks. Wasn't that easier than you thought?

1. Glue an inner-arc foundation and an outer-arc foundation to template plastic. Carefully cut the templates on the solid line with your paper scissors.

2. Lay the outer arc template on the *wrong* side of the fabric and trace around it with a pencil. Trace as many arcs as you need for your blocks. Repeat for the inner arcs.

3. Now it's time to put those blocks together. Fold the outer arc in half to find its center and place a pin there or pinch the fabric to make a crease. Do the same thing with the spiky unit (fig. 11).

4. Lay the spiky-unit fabric side up. Lay the outer arc on the spiky unit, right sides together, matching the pins or creases in the center. Place a pin through both pieces in the center then remove the matching pins, if used (fig. 12). Pin the two pieces together at each end and then in several places along the edge to be sewn.

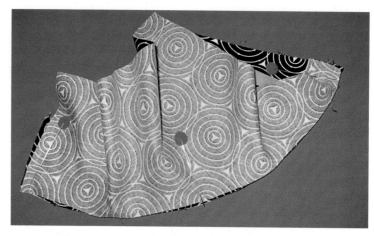

Fig. 12. Pin the curve in the middle and both ends. More pins can be added where desired.

5. With the stitch length at the normal setting (8–10 stitches per inch), sew slowly, paper side down, easing in the fullness of the outer arc as you go (fig. 13). Remove the pins. Turn the unit paper side up. Your stitches should be on or close to the sewing line. At both ends of the sewn line, the edges of the two pieces should match. Press the arc flat. Repeat this process for sewing the inner arc to the spiky unit.

"For a curved seam, we usually sew five to ten stitches; stop; and with the needle down, lift the presser foot and manually ease in any fullness; drop the foot again; sew five to ten more stitches and repeat the easing-in process. This method will ensure that there are no puckers or pleats in the curved piece." Deb and Janet

Fig. 13. Sew slowly with the foundation on the bottom.

6. Now you can remove the paper. Start with the little bits in the seam allowance, then remove the larger pieces, gently tearing along the perforated sewing lines. You don't want to rip or pull threads or distort your fabric. Square up your blocks, as needed.

A Word about Quilting

Once you're done piecing your beautiful quilt top, it's time to quilt it. We have found that quilting our own quilts enables us to maintain artistic control of how they will look when completed, and we love machine quilting. We do all of our quilting on our home sewing machines, not on a professional longarm machine.

You will see, as you read through the patterns and look at the quilting motifs, that we gather our inspiration from all aspects of life around us. Please feel free to copy what you see or draw your own wonderful designs. If you're like us, you might try checking your note pads around the house for doodles that would translate well into beautiful quilting motifs.

"Machine quilting is like handwriting. No two quilters stitch exactly alike, nor should they want to. Keep sewing and you will find your own voice via thread and pattern." Janet

We feel it is important to include the following basic guidelines to make the quilting process go smoothly for you.

The Workspace

It's important that the sewing surface be flat, so we suggest you use, or purchase if you need to, one of those extension tables that fits around your particular model of sewing machine.

For large quilts, you will need a large work surface. A dining room table is great for this, but make sure it is clean and dry before laying your quilt down on it. If you don't have a dining room table, we have found that putting your sewing table together with your ironing board (adjusted to the height of your sewing table) will also work well to carry the weight of the quilt. The larger the work surface, the less stress there is on the quilt. The weight of a quilt hanging down over a table edge can significantly slow the quilting process and inhibit your ability to move the quilt around comfortably while you're sewing. Keep the quilt up on the work surface.

In some cases, you might find it necessary to polish your work surface with a product appropriate for it to allow your quilt to glide smoothly at your machine.

Good lighting is essential for intricate work such as quilting, especially if you are free-motion quilting a marked quilting pattern. You cannot follow lines if you can't see them! We generally quilt free-motion without any marked lines, but we do need to see where we're going and where we've been. To avoid eyestrain, we have found that true daylight lighting works really well. Not only do you see clearly but the colors are true. You can find good daylight lighting at any hardware store or online.

Your Sewing Machine

Sewing machines should be regularly cleaned, oiled, and kept in good working order. Make sure you are using the appropriate presser foot for the type of quilting you are doing. You'll be going through more than one bobbin, so why keep stopping to wind them? Go ahead

and pre-wind about five to ten bobbins, depending on the quilt size and the density of your quilting style. Always start with a full bobbin when you begin quilting. You don't want to keep breaking your rhythm by constantly changing bobbins.

Needles are important as well. Dull needles will cause skipped stitches, broken or frayed threads, and uneven tension. Change your needles after, at most, every twelve to fifteen hours of quilting. We use topstitch needles, size 90; Metafil 80; quilting 75 or 90; or Stick-Nadel embroidery 90. Make sure you change your needles, if needed, when changing threads. Many of the new decorative metallic and Mylar threads require special needles, and they simply won't work well without them.

"Many of our students own sewing machines that cost thousands of dollars, yet they groan at the thought of replacing a $1.00 needle! Think about this for a minute … does this make sense to you? It certainly doesn't to us." Deb and Janet

Quilting

When you're ready to start quilting, take the time to make a small "sandwich" (10" x 10") from a fabric from the quilt top, the batting, and the backing. You are not only testing for correct tension, but you are also auditioning the thread you've chosen. Now is the time to make any and all necessary adjustments to the needle, thread, and tension to ensure good sewing. You can also play with quilting motifs, to see what might look best on your quilt.

Batting and Thread

With all the choices of wonderful battings and threads out there, your personal preferences should dictate what you choose for your quilts. Many quilters think that cotton is the preferred batting for quilts, and in many cases, it is, but there are always those quilts that need more loft (puffiness), and that is where the polyester-blend battings come in. We use both types. If your quilt is intended for a smooth flat wallhanging then, by all means, use cotton. If you choose something that will puff a bit more and really give dimension to your quilting, a wonderful cotton-poly blend may be the best choice for you.

With the seemingly endless possibility of threads out there, the choices can be daunting. Each quilt will have its own "life," so to speak, so we always debut a number of threads to find the perfect ones for our quilts. With a full range of colors available on the market, you will find the perfect color or colors to enhance your quilt.

Many quilters use Quilter's Gloves™ or rubber finger cots for traction when quilting. They find it helps them move the quilt around and maintain tautness. We don't because we prefer to feel the quilt beneath our hands, and we find that gloves or cots actually interfere with manipulating the quilt. In addition, we change threads and needles often for each quilt, and have found that gloves or cots slow us down. Try using these aids and then just using your fingers to see what works best for you.

Last but not least, practice, practice, practice! The more you quilt, the better you will get at it, and that's a fact!

chapter 2

Small Spiky Projects

H ere are three small projects to get
you started with paper piecing:
ROMAN HOLIDAY PLACEMAT (page 22),
PLAYFUL PLACEMAT (page 25), and RISE
AND SHINE PILLOWCASE (page 27).
All are easy and fun to do.

ROMAN HOLIDAY PLACEMAT

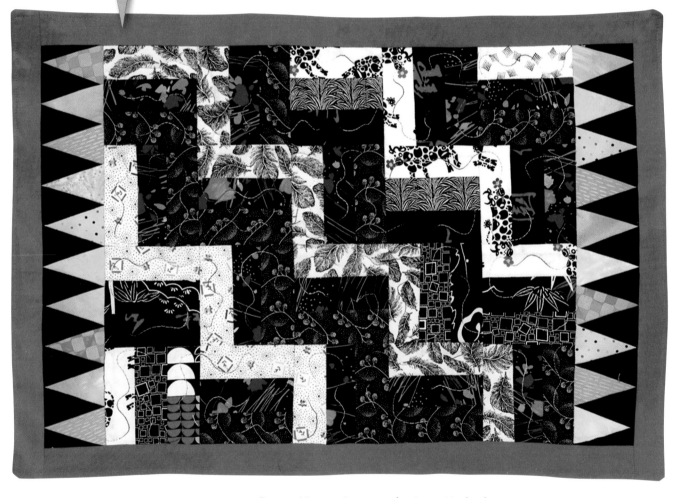

ROMAN HOLIDAY PLACEMAT, by Janet Mednick

Placemat size 14" x 21"
Blocks 3" x 3" finished.

Placemats are popular items to make when trying out a new pattern or technique. They don't require a large commitment of fabric or time when made in pairs or even in sets of four. You get to see if you like a design or fabric combo, and when they are done, you have a useful household item or gift.

ROMAN HOLIDAY was designed to go with BLACK TOOTH (page 39), which hangs in Janet's kitchen, but the placemat would be fun in any number of colorways. The simple spiked edge is quick to stitch and will really rev you up for our more adventurous projects.

Placemat Assembly

1. Print two spiky border foundations from the CD. Then, as they are needed, cut the fabric pieces listed in the materials table.

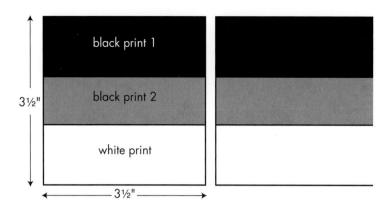

Fig. 1. Make 4 strip sets. Cut 5 squares for each.

2. Join two black-print strips and one white-print strip to make a strip-set (fig. 1). Make a total of four strip-sets. (Vary the prints in the strip-sets but keep them in the same order: black, black, white.) Cut the strip-sets into twenty 3½" squares.

3. Arrange the squares so they form a zigzag pattern, set four by five (see placemat photo). Sew the squares into rows then sew the rows together.

Materials for One Placemat	
Fabrics	**Cut**
Bright color ¼ yd.	20 spikes 2¼″ x 3″
Black ¼ yd.	22 backgrounds 2¼″ x 3″
Assorted black prints, scraps	8 strips 1½″ x 18″
Assorted white prints, scraps	4 strips 1½″ x 18″
Red border, ¼ yd.	4 strips 1½″ x 22″
Backing ½ yd.	1 panel 16″ x 23″
Thin batting	1 panel 16″ x 23″

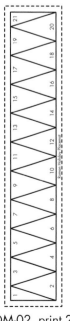

ROM-02, print 2

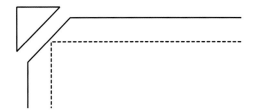

Fig. 2. Clip the corners to make them easier to turn.

4. Paper piece the two spiky borders, as described on page 14. Remove the paper. Sew a spiky border to each short side of the placemat.

5. Add red border strips to the two long sides and trim off any extra length. Add red border strips to the remaining sides and trim.

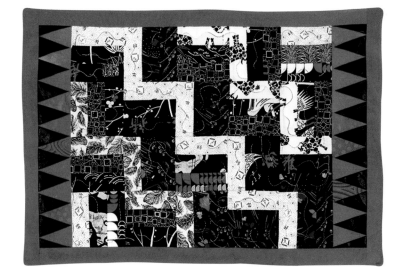

Envelope Finishing

1. Lay out the batting on a flat surface and place the backing on it, *right side up*. Center the pieced placemat on the backing, *right side down*. Pin around the edges through all the layers.

2. Sew ¼" in from the edge of the placemat top, leaving a 3" to 4" opening on a short side for turning. Trim the batting and backing even with the edges of the placemat top and clip the corners (fig. 2). Slip your hand between the top and the backing and turn the placemat right side out.

3. Fold in the seam allowances along the opening and press the folds. Stitch completely around the placemat approximately ³⁄₁₆" from the edge. This stitching will give you a nice finished edge while catching the seam allowances to close the opening.

4. Quilt the layers lightly. Too much dense quilting might distort the piece because the edges are already closed. Press.

"When we teach machine quilting for beginners, we suggest that our students make placemats for practicing their free-motion skills. Using one large-scale print for the placemat tops, students outline quilt the fabric's print. Many students excitedly reported back to us that they had made multiple sets of holiday gifts this way and improved their quilting, too!" Janet

A small spiky project done … unless you want to make a set of four. Go ahead. It doesn't take long!

PLAYFUL PLACEMAT

PLAYFUL PLACEMAT, by Deb Karasik

Placemat size: 13½" x 16"

This placemat is in Deb's kitchen. It is made of a basic spiky block stretched into an oval shape rather than a round one. With stretched blocks like this, you need to remember that there are two mirror images to sew.

Placemat Assembly

1. From the CD, print two foundations for each block. Cut the sections apart, leaving about ¼" extra paper around the outside of each one.

2. As they are needed, cut the fabric pieces listed in the materials table. Then piece four B units and four C units, as described in Sewing Spikes on page 14. Do not remove the paper yet.

3. For each block, sew unit A to unit B, gently easing unit A to fit. Sew unit D to unit C in the same manner.

4. Being careful not to pull the stitches, remove the paper from the backs of the C units.

5. Pin unit C at each spike tip to unit B. Sew the units together. Remove the paper from the B units. Join all the blocks.

6. Follow the instructions for envelope finishing on page 24 to layer and finish your placemat.

You now have a wonderful new placemat. These make great fun and easy gifts for friends and family.

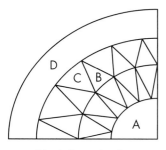

Block 1, make 2

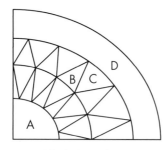

Block 2, make 2

Materials for One Placemat		
Fabrics	**Pieces**	**Cut**
Light blue ⅜ yd.	4 A	3" x 3½"
	20 B backgrounds	2¼" x 3"
	20 C spikes	2¼" x 3½"
Yellow ⅜ yd.	24 B spikes	1¾" x 2¾"
	24 C backgrounds	2¾" x 3½"
Medium blue ⅜ yd.	4 D	4¼" x 11½"
Backing 1 fat quarter	1 panel	15½" x 18"
Thin batting	1 panel	15½" x 18"

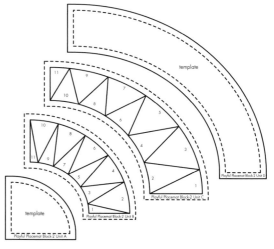

PLA-02 and PLA-03, print 2 of each block

RISE & SHINE PILLOWCASE

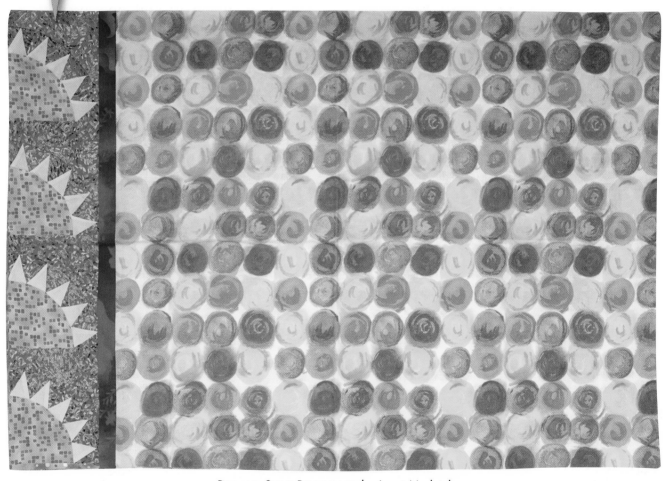

RISE AND SHINE PILLOWCASE, by Janet Mednick

Standard size: 20" x 29"

Blocks 5" x 5" finished.

Here's a small project that will allow you to test the waters by making a few spiky blocks. Pillowcases, usually made in theme printed fabrics, are popular gifts around our guild. We thought it would be fun to spike them up a bit!

Pillowcase Assembly

1. Print four block patterns from the CD. As they are needed, cut the fabric pieces listed in the materials table.

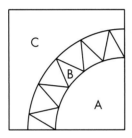

Block 1, make 4

Materials for One Placemat Use fabric at least 40½" wide. Cut strips selvage to selvage.	
Fabrics	**Cut**
Pillowcase body ¾ yd.	1 panel 24½" x 40½"
Red piping ¼ yd.	1 strip 2" x 40½"
Pillowcase hem ½ yd.	
hem 1	1 strip 5½" x 20½"
hem 2	1 strip 5½" x 40½"
Block unit A, scraps	4 squares 4" x 4"
Block unit B, scraps	20 spikes 2" x 2¼"
	24 backgrounds 2¼" x 2¼"
Block unit C, scraps	4 squares 6" x 6"

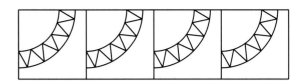

Fig. 1. Block row

2. Piece the four arcs as described on page 16. Sew the A pieces to the arcs then add the C pieces to complete the blocks.

3. Remove the paper. Sew the blocks together in a row (fig. 1).

4. Sew the hem-1 strip to one end of the blocks, as shown in figure 2.

5. Sew the hem-2 strip along the top edge of the block/hem-1 unit, right sides together (fig. 3). Fold hem 2 to the back and press to complete the block section.

6. Fold the piping strip in half along its length, wrong sides together, and press.

7. Align the raw edges of the piping strip with the raw edges of the block section, on the right side. Baste the raw edges together through all four layers.

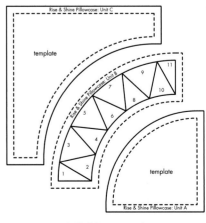

RIS-02, print 4

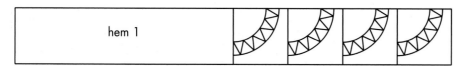

Fig. 2. Block/hem 1 unit

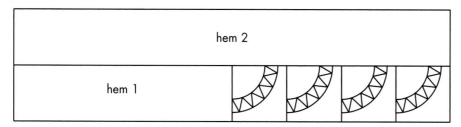

Fig. 3. Adding hem 2

8. Fold the pillowcase body in half, aligning the 24½" edges, and press the fold to mark the center.

9. To join the block section to the pillowcase body, align the raw edges of both pieces, right sides together. Be sure to match the block/hem-1 seam with the pillowcase body fold. Pin in place.

10. Sew with a ¼" seam allowance through all the layers. If necessary, trim the block section even with the sides of the pillowcase body. Fold out the block section and press (fig. 4). Press the piping toward the block section.

11. Fold the pillowcase on the centerline, right sides together, matching the block section seam lines.

12. Sew down the long raw edge and across the bottom (fig. 5). You can add a zigzag stitch to finish the seam allowances, if desired. Turn the pillowcase right side out and iron. Voila, you're done!

That was fun, wasn't it? Are you ready to make another pillowcase? Or try the next project.

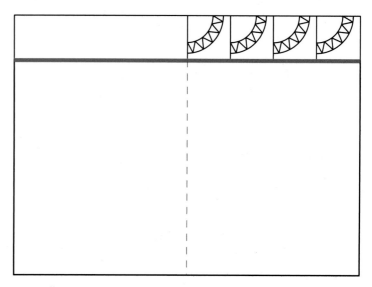

Fig. 4. Pillowcase with blocks and piping attached

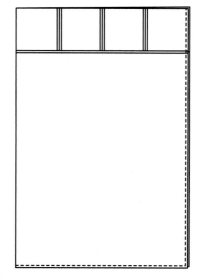

Fig. 5. Sew the side and bottom edges.

chapter 3

Wickedly Easy Spikes

The three projects in this section may appear to be more challenging, but by simply following the paper-piecing techniques presented on pages 11–17, you will enjoy making these spiky gems.

ROLLING SPIRALS

ROLLING SPIRALS, by Deb Karasik

Quilt size 38" x 38"
Blocks 8" x 8" finished

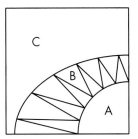

Colorway 1, make 8
Colorway 2, make 8

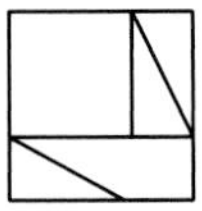

Rolling Spirals and Autumn Calls, page 93, are made from the same block, but the changes in the colors, block arrangements, and borders make them look totally different.

Border block 1, make 4

Note: The measurements for precutting spike and background fabrics are based on the largest spike dimensions. If you would prefer to conserve fabric, see Precutting Fabrics on page 13.

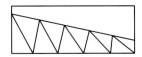

Border block 2, make 16

Yardage & Cutting
Use fabric at least 40" wide.
Cut strips selvage to selvage.

Fabrics	Pieces	Cut
Black print 1¾ yd.	8 A	4½" x 4½"
	56 B backgrounds	2¾" x 5¼"
	8 C	9" x 9"
border	44 spikes	2½" x 4"
White print 1¾ yd.	8A	4½" x 4½"
	56 B backgrounds	2¾" x 5¼"
	8 C	9" x 9"
border	44 spikes	2½" x 4"
Dark red ½ yd.	48 B spikes	2" x 5¼"
Yellow ½ yd.	48 B spikes	2" x 5¼"
Red border 1¼ yd.	88 backgrounds	2½" x 4"
	16 border piece #11	3¼" x 9¼"
	4 corner piece #1	3" x 3"
Backing 1¼ yd.	1 panel	42" x 42"
Batting	1 panel	42" x 42"
Binding ½ yd.	5 strips	2½" x 40"

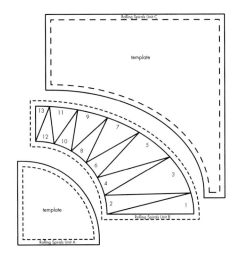

ROL-02, print 16

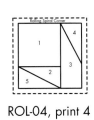

ROL-04, print 4

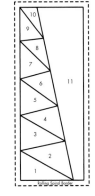

ROL-03, print 16

Note: Patterns are reversed so finished pieces will be oriented like photo.

Assembly

1. Print the foundations for sixteen blocks, sixteen border units, and four corner units from the CD. As they are needed, cut the fabric pieces listed in the yardage & cutting table.

2. Referring to Sewing Spikes (page 14) and Sewing Arcs (page 16), make eight blocks in colorway 1 and eight in colorway 2. Remove the paper foundations.

3. Square up your blocks, if necessary, so they are all 8½" x 8½", which includes seam allowances.

4. Look at the quilt photo and arrange your blocks accordingly. Sew the blocks together in rows then join the rows.

5. Paper piece the border units just like you pieced the blocks. Remember to piece eight units with black spikes and eight with white spikes. Remove the paper.

6. Arrange the border units around the finished blocks as shown in the quilt photo. Join the units to form four border strips.

7. Sew two of these border strips to opposite sides of the quilt top.

8. Paper piece the four corner units and sew one on each end of the two remaining border strips. Add these border strips to the top and bottom of the quilt.

9. Layer the quilt top, batting, and backing; baste. Quilt the layers, referring to our suggested quilted ideas on page 18 if you need inspiration. Then bind the raw edges to complete your quilt.

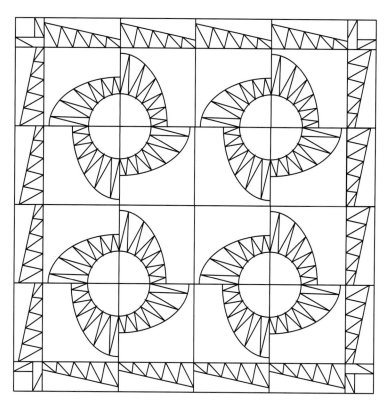

Assembly diagram

AARON'S QUILT II

AARON'S QUILT II, by Deb Karasik

Quilt size 40" x 40"

Large blocks 10" x 10" finished

Small blocks 5" x 5" finished

This is one of the most popular classes we teach. Students love to play with the colors to make this fresh, spiky quilt. The split spikes look more difficult, but guess what? They're not.

Yardage	
Use fabric at least 40½" wide.	
Fabrics	**Yards**
Red	⅝
Purple	⅜
Yellow	¾
Teal	2⅛
Navy	1½
Orange	1⅝
Backing	2¾
Binding	½

See cutting chart on page 36.

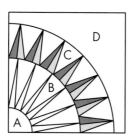

Large block, make 4

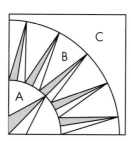

Small block, make 8

Assembly

1. Print four large and eight small block patterns and four border strip patterns from the CD to use as foundations. As they are needed, cut the pieces listed in the cutting table on page 36.

2. Referring to Sewing Spikes (page 14) and Sewing Arcs (page 16), make the blocks shown in the block diagrams. Remove the paper foundations.

3. Square up your blocks, if necessary. The large ones should measure 10½" x 10½" and the small ones 5½" x 5½", which includes seam allowances.

4. Refer to the quilt photo and arrange your blocks, sashing strips, cornerstones, and side and corner triangles. Sew the pieces together in diagonal rows then join the rows.

5. Paper piece the border strips then remove the paper. Sew two border strips to opposite sides of the quilt top.

6. Sew a corner square to each end of the two remaining border strips then add them to the top and bottom of the quilt.

7. Layer the quilt top, batting, and backing; baste. Quilt the layers, referring to our suggested quilting ideas on page 18 if you need inspiration. Then bind the raw edges to complete your quilt.

Cutting Use fabric at least 40" wide. Cut strips selvage to selvage.		
Fabrics	**Pieces**	**Cut**
Large block		
purple	24 B spikes	1½" x 5"
	28 C split spikes	1½" x 4"
red	4 A	3" x 3"
	28 C split spikes	1½" x 4"
teal	32 C backgrounds	3" x 4"
	4 D	11" x 11"
yellow	28 B backgrounds	2½" x 5"
Small block		
navy	16 A backgrounds	2½" x 2¾"
	48 B backgrounds	2½" x 3½"
	8 C	6" x 6"
red	8 A split spikes	1½" x 3¼"
	40 B split spikes	1½" x 3½"
yellow	8 A split spikes	1½" x 3¼"
	40 B split spikes	1½" x 3½"
Other pieces		
navy	8 E sashes	2½" x 10½"
	4 accent border strips	1½" x 38½"
red	5 F cornerstones	2¼" x 2¼"
	4 G half cornerstones	one 3¾" square cut in quarters diagonally
	4 H quarter cornerstones	two 2⅛" squares cut in half diagonally
yellow	8 E sashes	2¼" x 10½"
orange	16 I side triangles	four 8⅜" squares cut in quarters diagonally
	128 border spikes	2¼" x 3¼"
	4 J border corner squares	2½" x 2½"
teal	132 border backgrounds	2¼" x 3¼"
Backing	2 panels	24" x 46"
Batting	1 panel	46" x 46"
Binding	5 strips	2½" x 40"

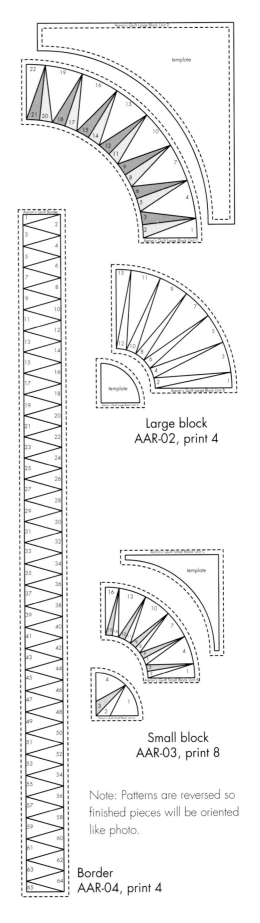

Large block
AAR-02, print 4

Small block
AAR-03, print 8

Note: Patterns are reversed so finished pieces will be oriented like photo.

Border
AAR-04, print 4

Appliquéing the A Unit

LARGE BLOCK

Because the center arc is so small, it's much easier to use a simple appliqué technique to machine sew unit A to unit B.

✦ Trace the A unit on the dull side of a piece of freezer paper. Cut the freezer-paper template on the sewing line (yes, cut off the seam allowance).

✦ Iron the freezer-paper template onto the wrong side of your 3" fabric square. Carefully cut the fabric piece, adding a ¼" allowance by eye as you cut (fig 1).

✦ Dab a glue stick on the curved edge of the allowance only and finger press the allowance to the back, over the freezer paper. Make sure you keep the curve nice and curvy, without any little peaks or points (fig. 2).

✦ Carefully align unit A over unit B. Using thread that matches the A unit as closely as possible, machine sew the edge with a small straight or zigzag stitch. Now remove the freezer paper. See? Wasn't that a piece of cake?

SMALL BLOCK

This same technique can be used to appliqué the small block's A unit. Paper piece the A unit as usual. Then cut a unit-A template out of freezer paper. Iron the freezer-paper template to the back of unit A and appliqué it to the B unit as described for the large block.

This technique will take any stress out of trying to set in such small curves. However, you will quickly become addicted to these spiky quilts and become an expert in setting in curves no matter how small. But for now, let's just use this technique and get this quilt done.

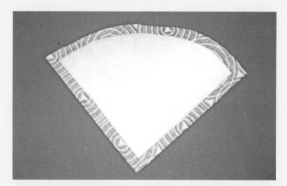

Fig. 1. Cutting the fabric piece

Fig. 2. Turn the allowance over the freezer paper.

Assembly diagram

BLACK TOOTH

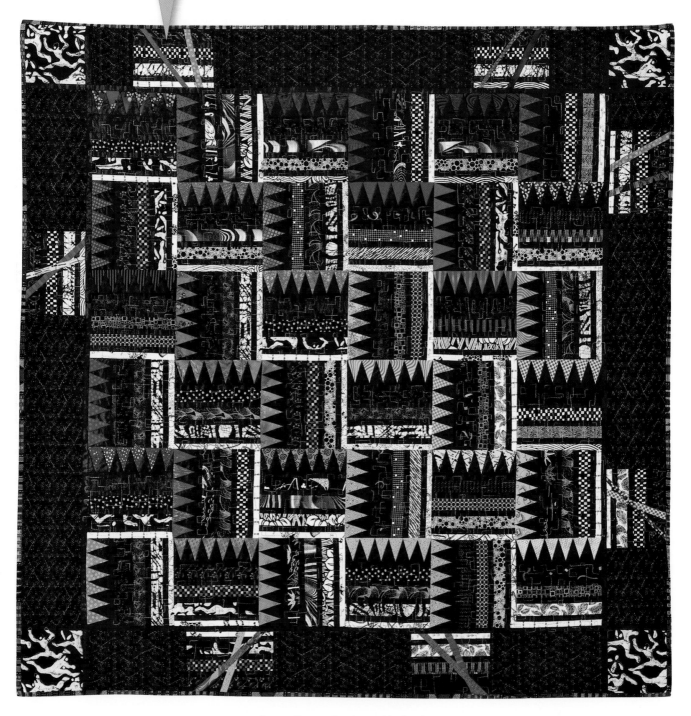

BLACK TOOTH, by Janet Mednick

Quilt size 57" x 57"

Blocks 7½" x 7½" finished

When we recarpeted the house, I had to empty my sewing room. Can you imagine? In the process, I discovered quite a collection of black and white fabrics. Deciding that they needed to be used, I started designing a basic Rail Fence pattern with added spikes. After sewing the first few blocks, it was clear they were boring. I just couldn't make an all black and white quilt; I had to have color! Adding vivid color to some strips and all the spikes made the blocks sing.

The blocks pieced into the outer border were ones I had accidentally cut too small and had put aside. They came in handy when I wanted something fun in the border, don't you think?

Block Assembly

1. Print 36 spike foundations from the CD. As they are needed, cut the fabric pieces listed in the yardage and cutting table.

2. Using the precut spike and background fabric rectangles, paper piece the spike units.

3. Sew one solid black strip to each of the eight white with black strips and each of the 24 black with white strips (fig. 1, page 41).

4. Sew the pairs into a strip-set as arranged in figure 2. Make eight strip-sets.

5. Cut the strip-sets into forty 6" wide segments. Use 36 for the quilt body and set four aside for the outer border, if you like.

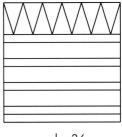

make 36

Yardage & Cutting
Use fabric at least 40" wide.
Cut strips selvage to selvage, except the outer border.

Fabrics	Yards	Cut
Assorted white with black prints, strip-sets	⅜ total	8 strips 1" x 40"
Assorted black with white prints, strip-sets	1⅛ total	24 strips 1½" x 40"
Black solid, strip-sets	2⅝	32 strips 1" x 40"
paper piecing		252 backgrounds 2¼" x 3¼"
inner border		6 strips 1" x 40"
Assorted colors, paper piecing	1¼ total	216 spikes 2¼" x 3¼"
Black print, outer border	1½	4 strips 6" x 45½" (cut lengthwise)
Black and white print, outer border corners	¼	4 squares 6" x 6"
Backing	3⅝	2 panels 33" x 63"
Batting		63" x 63"
Binding	⅝	7 strips 2½"

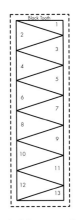

BLA-02, print 36

6. Sew the spike units to the strip-pieced segments with the bases of the black teeth next to the black solid strips. Remove the paper.

7. Arrange the blocks, set six by six, as shown in the photo. Sew the blocks together in rows then sew the rows together.

8. The quilt should measure 45½" square, including seam allowances. If it doesn't, adjust the widths of the seam allowances between the blocks as necessary.

Borders and Finishing

Now you get to decide whether to piece the extra blocks into the outer border or keep your border simple. It's up to you.

For our quilt, we slashed the extra blocks and stitched strips of color into them for fun. Then we randomly set the blocks into our outer border strips. Try this or try something else. It's your turn to play!

1. Set the extra blocks into the four outer border strips and trim the resulting borders to 45½" in length.

2. Sew the six inner border strips together, end to end, with diagonal seams to make one long strip.

3. Cut two strips 45½" long from the long strip. Sew these strips to the sides of the quilt then add the outer border strips to the sides of the quilt. Your quilt, with the borders, should be 57½" wide.

4. Cut two strips 57½" from the long inner border strip. Sew these to the top and bottom of the quilt.

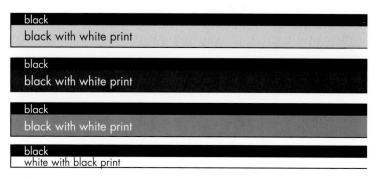

Fig. 1. Sew strips into pairs.

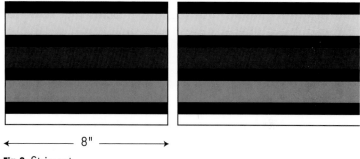

← 8" →

Fig. 2. Strip-set

5. Cut four 6" strips from the long inner border strip. Sew a 6" strip and a corner square to each end of the remaining outer border strips then sew the border strips to the top and bottom of the quilt.

6. Layer the quilt top, batting, and backing; baste. Quilt the layers then bind the raw edges to complete your quilt.

"The quilting in Blacktooth *is an allover meander of straight lines forming overlapping squares and rectangles. There's no quilting in the teeth. The border fabric had a pattern of red dots, which I connected zigzag style, forming quilted diamonds."*
Janet

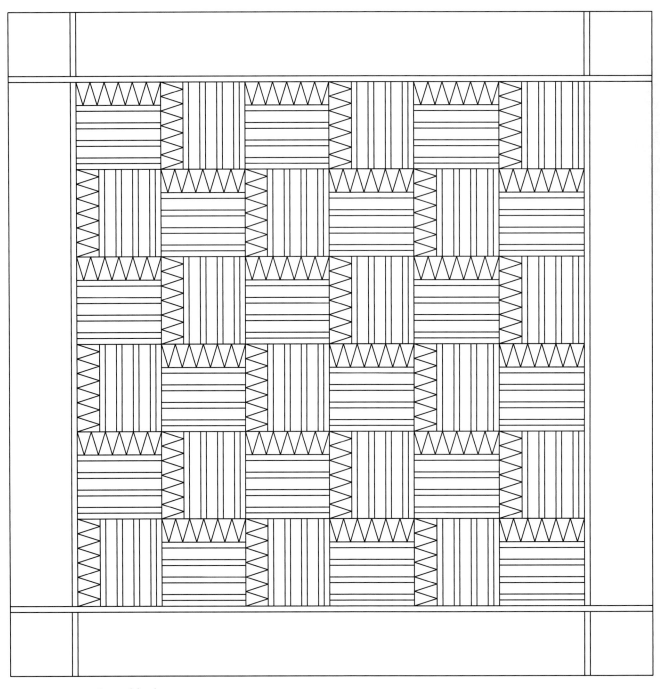

Assembly diagram

chapter 4

*A*bandoning the Traditional

Now that you've explored basic spikes and split spikes, are you ready for the next step? Sure you are! Now you can try some blocks that will amaze your friends with their complex visual appeal. Not to worry, they are just as easy to sew as the basic spiky blocks, but you will need to give a bit more thought to the fabrics that go into making them.

DAY AT THE BEACH

DAY AT THE BEACH, by Deb Karasik

Quilt size 48" x 48"

Blocks 10" x 10" finished

This is a fabulous quilt for using up scraps. Every outer block has a different set of fabrics and colors. The dark blue in the center and inner border holds it all together, so you can play in your stash and scrap baskets, mixing and matching the colors any way you want.

This pattern features split spikes, which really aren't any harder to make than one-piece spikes. They do add a few more seams and more time to the sewing process, but they also add more dimension in return. The spike arcs are a bit skewed, adding interesting movement to the setting.

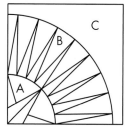

Inner block, make 4

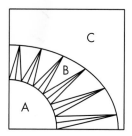

Outer block, make 12

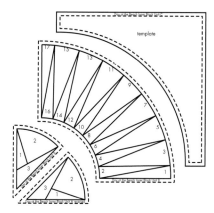

Inner block, DAY-02, print 4

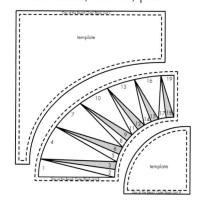

Outer block, DAY-03, print 12

Note: Patterns are reversed so finished pieces will be oriented like photo.

Yardage & Cutting
Use fabric at least 40" wide.
Cut strips selvage to selvage.

Fabrics	Pieces	Cut
Navy 2⅛ yd. inner block	8 A backgrounds	3½" x 3½"
	4 C	11" x 11"
	36 B backgrounds	2¾" x 6"
outer block	12 A	5¼" x 5¼"
inner border	5 strips	1½" x 40"
binding	6 strips	2½" x 40"
Scraps 4 ⅜ yds. total inner block	16 A spikes	2" x 5"
	32 B spikes	2" x 6"
outer block	144 B split spikes	1½" x 6½"
	84 B backgrounds	3¼" x 6½"
	12 C	11" x 11"
Outer border ⅝ yds.	5 strips	3½" x 40"
Backing 3 yds.	2 panels	28" x 53"
Batting	1 panel	53" x 53"

Assembly

1. Print four inner and twelve outer block foundations from the CD.

2. Referring to Sewing Spikes (page 14) and Sewing Arcs (page 16), make four inner blocks.

3. For the outer-block B units, sort the colors into twelve combinations that please you, making sure there's contrast between the spikes and the background. Each set should include two colors for the split spikes and one color for the background.

4. Sew the twelve B units then add the A units. Audition the A/B units with the unit-C fabrics you've chosen. Once you are satisfied with the colors, sew the A/B units to the C units.

5. Remove the paper foundations from the inner and outer blocks. Square up your blocks, if necessary, so they are 10½", which includes seam allowances.

6. Arrange the inner and outer blocks as seen in the quilt photo and sew them together in rows. Then join the rows.

7. Sew the inner border strips together, end to end, with diagonal seams to make one long strip. Using your quilt's measurements, cut two strips from the long strip and sew these to the sides of the quilt.

8. In this same way, measure, cut, and sew strips to the top and bottom of the quilt. Use this same method to add the outer borders.

9. Layer the quilt top, batting, and backing; baste. Quilt the layers. Refer to our suggested quilting ideas on page 18 if you need inspiration. Then bind the raw edges to complete your quilt.

"We like to cut borders after the blocks have been sewn together and we have auditioned a few different border fabrics to see which one really works. It's almost impossible to know whether your fabric choice will really sing in tune with and bring out the beauty of a quilt top until the end. So save yourselves time and money and wait." Janet

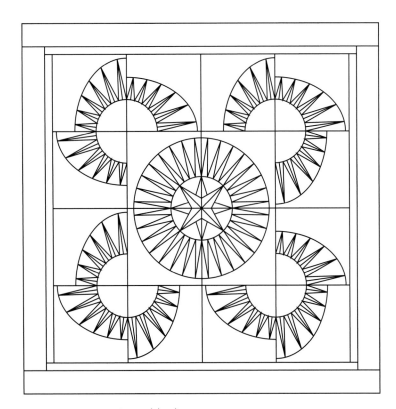

Assembly diagram

WHIRLIGIG

WHIRLIGIG, by Deb Karasik

Quilt size 53" x 53"

Blocks 10" x 10" finished

Border blocks 5" x 5" finished

I designed this quilt for a class project for students who had already taken several classes with me and were craving something more. When they first saw it, they feared they had bitten off more than they could chew, but early on, they discovered what fun these blocks are to make.

The delightful part of this quilt is the movement created by the spikes. Have fun choosing your fabrics, and remember that changing the colors of the blocks will help you get the glow you want in this quilt.

Yardage	
Use fabric at least 40" wide.	
Fabrics	**Yards**
Dark blue	4⅝
Light blue print	1½
Red, with binding	⅞
Scraps	2½ total
Backing	3½

See cutting chart on page 49.

*N*ote: *The measurements for precutting spike and background fabrics are based on the dimensions of the largest pieces. If you would rather conserve fabric, see Precutting Fabrics on page 13.*

Assembly

1. Print the following foundations from the CD: four block 1, twelve block 2, four border blocks, and four reversed border blocks. As they are needed, cut the fabric pieces listed in the cutting table.

2. Referring to Sewing Spikes (page 14) and Sewing Arcs (page 16), make the blocks shown in the diagrams. Remove the paper foundations.

3. Square up your blocks, if necessary, so that blocks 1 and 2 are 10½" x 10½" and the border blocks are 5½" x 5½", which includes seam allowances.

4. Look at the quilt photo and arrange blocks 1 and 2 accordingly. Sew the blocks together in rows then join the rows.

5. Sew the inner border strips together, end to end with diagonal seams, to make one continuous strip. Using your quilt's measurements, cut two side border strips from the continuous strip. Sew them to the quilt. Repeat for the top and bottom borders.

6. Sew the border blocks together in pairs, as shown in figure 1, page 50.

7. Sew a block pair between two 17" outer border strips (fig. 2, page 50). Repeat. Sew these strips to the sides of the quilt and trim off any extra border length.

8. Sew a block pair between two 22" outer border strips. Repeat. Sew these strips to the top and bottom of the quilt and trim.

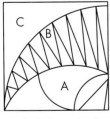

Block 1, make 4

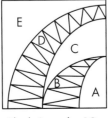

Block 2, make 12

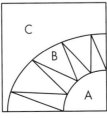

Border block, make 8

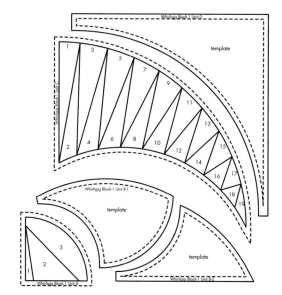

Block 1, WHI-02, print 4

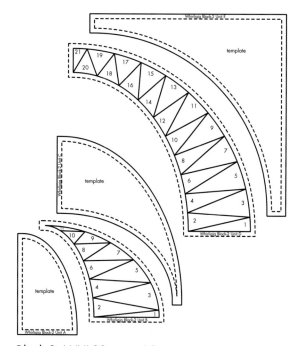

Block 2, WHI-03, print 12

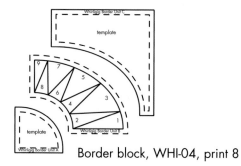

Border block, WHI-04, print 8

Note: Patterns are reversed so finished pieces will be oriented like photo.

Cutting
Use fabric at least 40" wide.
Cut strips selvage to selvage.

Fabrics	Pieces	Cut
Block 1		
dark blue print	40 C backgrounds	2½" x 7¼"
	4 D	11" x 11"
	4 B, piece #2	5" x 8"
scraps	12 A	2½" x 6"
	4 B, piece #1	5" x 8"
	36 C spikes	2¼" x 7¼"
Block 2		
dark blue print	12 A	3½" x 5½"
	72 B backgrounds	2½" x 4¾"
	12 C	7¼" x 9"
	132 D backgrounds	2½" x 4¼"
	12 E	11" x 11"
scraps	60 B spikes	2" x 4½"
	120 D spikes	2" x 4½"
Border block		
scraps	32 B spikes	1¾" x 3¾"
light blue print	8 A	3" x 3"
	40 B backgrounds	2½" x 3¾"
	8 C	6" x 6"
Borders & binding		
red	5 inner border strips	2" x 40"
	6 binding strips	2½" x 40"
light blue print	4 outer border strips	5½" x 17"
	4 outer border strips	5½" x 22"
Backing	2 panels	30" x 59"
Batting	1 panel	59" x 59"

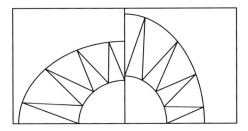

Fig. 1. ABOVE, Border block pair

Fig. 2. LEFT, Side border unit

9. Layer the quilt top, batting, and backing; baste. Quilt the layers. (Refer to our suggested quilting ideas on page 18 if you need inspiration.) Then bind the raw edges to complete your quilt.

"Because this quilt has so much motion with all the circular elements, try using a number of different threads for the quilting. It's an easy quilt to go crazy on and have a lot of fun." Deb

Assembly diagram

RASPBERRY SORBET

RASPBERRY SORBET, by Deb Karasik and Janet Mednick

Quilt size 43" x 43"
Blocks 9" x 9" finished

This quilt was designed in response to the clamorous requests of our fellow guild members and students for more: more classes, more color, more piecing variations to play with. Its rainbow-sherbet colors seem preplanned, but RASPBERRY SORBET is a scrap quilt of sorts.

It reads yellow, pink, and green, but look closely. You'll see there are multiple fabrics used for each color, once again a result of raiding the stash. There are some pink fabrics, for example, that are so close in color they appear, at first glance, to be the same fabric.

The degree of difficulty is raised here a bit because two of the three pieced blocks contain three sections requiring paper piecing. We just see this as more opportunity to play, both with colors and fabrics.

Yardage Use fabric at least 40" wide.	
Fabrics	**Yards**
Dark green	½
Medium green	⅝
Light green-1	½
Light green-2	¼
Orange	1⅛
Raspberry	2
Red	¼
Scraps	1⅛ total
Teal	¼
Yellow-1	¾
Yellow-2	⅝
Backing	2⅞
Binding	½

See cutting chart on page 53.

Note: The measurements for precutting spike and background fabrics are based on the dimensions of the largest pieces. If you would rather conserve fabric, see Precutting Fabrics on page 13.

Assembly

1. Print the following foundations from the CD: four block 1, eight block 2, and four block 3. As they are needed, cut the fabric pieces listed in the cutting table on page 53.

Because of the large variety of fabrics and colors in this quilt, we suggest you piece all the sections of block 1 before you cut the fabric pieces for block 2, etc. This will most definitely minimize the possibility of mixing up your various stacks of little pieces.

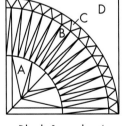

Block 1, make 4

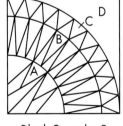

Block 2, make 8

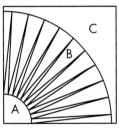

Block 3, make 4

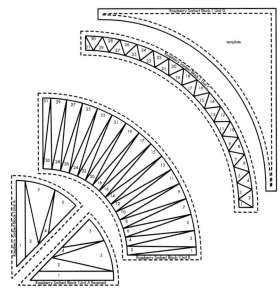

Block 1, RAS-02 print 4

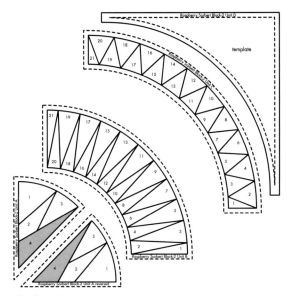

Block 2, RAS-03 print 8

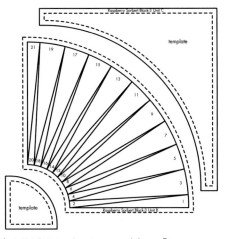

Block 3, RAS-04 print 4

Cutting Cut strips selvage to selvage.		
Fabrics	**Pieces**	**Cut**
Block 1		
scraps	16 A spikes	1½" x 5"
	24 A backgrounds	2½" x 5½"
yellow-1	60 B spikes	1¼" x 4½"
raspberry	64 B backgrounds	1¾" x 4½"
teal	64 C spikes	1½" x 1½"
red	60 C backgrounds	1½" x 1½"
light green-1	4 D	10" x 10"
Block 2		
scraps	32 A spikes	2" x 5½"
	32 A backgrounds	2¾" x 3¾"
dark green	80 B spikes	1¾" x 4"
orange	80 C backgrounds	2" x 4"
	88 C spikes	2" x 2¾"
yellow-2	80 C backgrounds	2½" x 2¾"
raspberry	8 D	10" x 10"
Block 3		
light green-1	4 A	3" x 3"
yellow-1	40 B spikes	1¼" x 7¼"
raspberry	44 B backgrounds	2¼" x 7¼"
	4 C	10" x 10"
Borders		
light green-2	4 inner border strips	1½" x 40"
medium green	5 outer border strips	3" x 40"
Backing	2 panels	22" x 49"
Batting	1 panel	40" x 49"
Binding	5 strips	2½" x 40"

Note: Patterns are reversed so finished pieces will be oriented like photo.

2. Referring to Sewing Spikes (page 14) and Sewing Arcs (page 16), make the blocks shown in the block diagrams. Remove the paper foundations.

3. Square up your blocks, if necessary, so they measure 9½" x 9½", which includes seam allowances.

4. Look at the quilt photo and arrange the blocks accordingly. Sew the blocks together in rows then join the rows.

5. Sew an inner border strip to the sides of the quilt and trim the strips even with the quilt's edges. Add the top and bottom inner border strips and trim.

6. Sew the outer border strips together, end to end with diagonal seams, to make one continuous strip. Using your quilt's measurements, cut two side border strips from the continuous strip. Sew them to the quilt. Repeat for the top and bottom borders.

7. Layer the quilt top, batting, and backing; baste. Quilt the layers. (Refer to our suggested quilting ideas on page 18 if you need inspiration.) Then bind the raw edges to complete your quilt.

"This is a perfect opportunity to use those fabulous mottled batiks that change color from section to section, but be sure to stay within a color family. In this quilt, a pink-peach-orange water batik was used, and it reads differently in various parts of the quilt. One fabric yielded three to four colorplays. Such a deal!" Janet and Deb

Assembly diagram

chapter 5

Extreme Spiking

Our next step on our creative journey was to test the waters by experimenting with unusual settings for spiky blocks. The first block looked great on paper, and we figured how hard could it be to make? Well, once you go into skewing blocks, there are some things that have to be considered. First of all, and most important, elongating blocks causes a lot of bias edges, which stretch out of shape easily. Starching the fabrics before cutting them helps control this, but you still have to be careful handling these blocks.

SPIKE REDUX

SPIKE REDUX, by Deb Karasik and Janet Mednick

Quilt size- 45" x 45"

Diamond blocks 11¼"
  on a side, finished

Corner blocks 11¼" x 11¼" finished

Border blocks 2½" x 8" finished

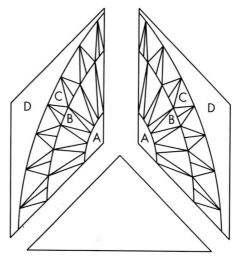

Diamond blocks and setting triangle,
make 4 each

The layout for this quilt was inspired by the Ohio Star block. There are eight diamond blocks inset with four setting triangles and four corner blocks. Remember to handle them with care and sew them with precision. Even slight imperfections or "wonkiness" can cause fitting problems when it comes to sewing the entire top together.

Corner block, make 4

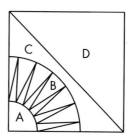

Border unit-1, make 4

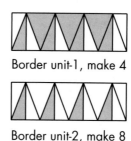

Border unit-2, make 8

Yardage	
Use fabric at least 40" wide.	
Fabrics	**Yards**
Aqua	⅞
Dark blue	2⅞
Dark purple	⅞
Light green	⅞
Medium orange-1	1½
Medium orange-2	¼
Multi-print	¼
Red orange	⅞
Yellow	½
Binding	⅝
Backing	3¼

See cutting chart on page 58.

Note: The measurements for precutting spike and background fabrics are based on the dimensions of the largest pieces. If you would rather conserve fabric for the diamond block, see Precutting Fabrics on page 13.

Assembly

1. Print the following foundations from the CD: four diamond blocks, four diamond blocks reversed, four corner blocks, and 12 border units.. As they are needed, cut the fabric pieces listed in the cutting table, page 58.

Cutting
Cut strips selvage to selvage.

Fabrics	Pieces	Cut
Diamond blocks		
aqua	8 A	2½" x 6½"
yellow	48 B spikes	1¾" x 5¾"
dark blue	56 B backgrounds	2½" x 6¼"
	4 setting triangles	Use template on CD.
light green	56 C split spikes	2" x 4½"
red orange	56 C split spikes	2" x 4½"
medium orange-1	8 D	6" x 24"
dark purple	64 C backgrounds	3½" x 4¾"
Corner block		
dark blue	4 A	4" x 4"
	28 B backgrounds	2¾" x 5"
	4 C backgrounds	4" x 18"
multi-print	24 B spikes	1½" x 5"
aqua	4 D	Use template on CD.
Inner border		
medium orange-2	4 strips	1¼" x 40"
aqua	4 corner squares	1¼" x 1¼"
Outer border		
light green	48 split spikes	2" x 3¾"
red orange	48 split spikes	2" x 3¾"
dark blue	48 backgrounds	3" x 3¾"
	4 corner squares	3" x 3"
	8 rectangles	3" x 8½"
aqua	12 backgrounds	3" x 3¾"
Backing	2 panels	27" x 54"
Batting	1 panel	54" x 54"
Binding	6 strips	2½" x 40"

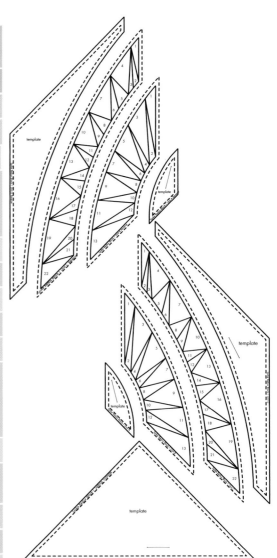

Diamond blocks and setting triangle,
SPI-02 print 4 each

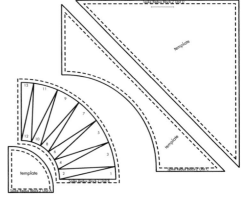

Corner block, SPI-03 print 4

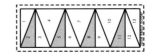

Border unit, SPI-04, print 12

Note: Patterns are reversed so finished pieces
will be oriented like photo.

2. Referring to Sewing Spikes (page 14) and Sewing Arcs (page 16), make the blocks shown in the block diagrams. Remove the paper foundations.

3. Square up the corner blocks, if needed, to 11¾" x 11¾", which includes seam allowances. The border units should measure 3" x 8½".

"It's time to join the blocks. We found that sewing this quilt together just as you would a Lone Star was the solution to making it work." Deb and Janet

4. Sew the center blocks together as shown in figure 1. Then add the setting triangles and corner blocks with set-in seams.

Fig. 1. Quilt assembly

Fig. 2. Outer border strip (note the aqua background in the middle unit)

5. Measure the width of your quilt and trim two inner border strips to this measurement. Add aqua corner squares to each end of both strips then set them aside.

6. Sew the remaining two border strips to the sides of the quilt and trim them even with the quilt's edges. Sew the border strips from step 5 to the top and bottom of the quilt.

7. To make an outer border strip, sew three border units and two rectangles as shown in figure 2. (If necessary, you can adjust for your quilt's measurements by resizing the rectangles.) Make four border strips like this.

8. Sew two of the border strips to the sides of the quilt. Then sew dark blue corner squares to the ends of the remaining border strips. Sew these strips to the top and bottom.

9. Layer the quilt top, batting, and backing; baste. Quilt the layers, referring to our suggested quilting ideas on page 18 if you need inspiration. Then bind the raw edges to complete your quilt.

PASSION IN THE ROUND

PASSION IN THE ROUND, by Janet Mednick

Quilt size 48" x 48"

Diamond blocks 9" on a side finished

Passion in the Round represents yet another step toward more intriguing (to us) designs based on a diamond block. Adding a second arc of spikes within an area that usually contains only one spike-set created a whole new sense of circular motion.

The two spike sections (B and C) are pieced in gradations of color. We used eight different fabrics for the spikes in unit C. In unit B, twelve different rust-to-yellow fabrics were used; one for each spike.

If laying out color gradations is not as fascinating to you as it is to us, by all means choose just one fabric that speaks to you. Or choose two or three that are similar in color but have different textures.

Yardage Use fabric at least 40" wide.	
Fabrics	**Yards**
Green	1
Light to medium blues	⅝ total
Medium blue	3¼
Orange	¼
Yellow to orange to rust scraps	1⅝ total
Rust	⅞
Inner border	⅜
Outer border	½
Backing	3¼
Binding	⅝

See cutting chart on page 63.

Note: The measurements for precutting spike and background fabrics are based on the dimensions of the largest pieces. If you would rather conserve fabric, see Precutting Fabrics on page 13.

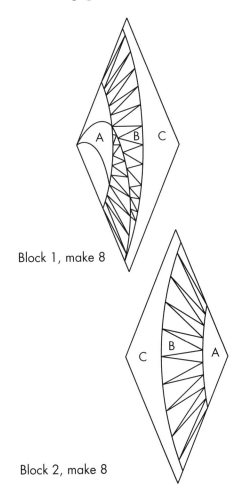

Block 1, make 8

Block 2, make 8

Assembly

1. From the CD, print eight foundations for block 1 and eight for block 2. As they are needed, cut the fabric pieces listed in the cutting table.

2. Referring to Sewing Spikes (page 14) and Sewing Arcs (page 16), make the blocks shown in the block diagrams. Remove the paper foundations. The diamonds should measure 9" on a side plus ¼" all around for seam allowances.

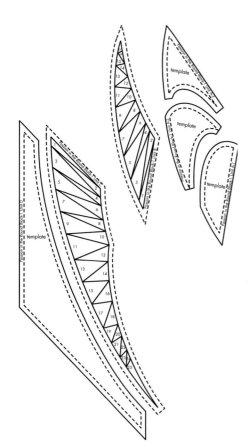

Block 1, PAS-03 print 8

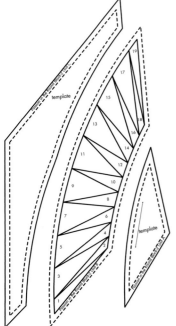

Block 2, PAS-02 print 8

Note: Patterns are reversed so finished pieces will be oriented like photo.

Cutting
Cut strips selvage to selvage.

Fabrics	Pieces	Cut
Block 1		
green	104 C backgrounds	2¼" x 4¾"
light to medium blues	72 B backgrounds	1¾" x 4¾"
medium blue	8 A-1	2¼" x 6"
	8 A-3	3" x 6"
yellow, orange, rust scraps	64 B spikes	1¼" x 4¾"
	96 C spikes	1¾" x 4½"
orange	8 A-2	3½" x 5"
rust	8 D	4½" x 19"
Block 2		
medium blue	80 B backgrounds	2¾" x 5½"
	8 C	4½" x 19"
rust	8 A	3" x 9"
yellow, orange, rust scraps	72 B spikes	1¾" x 5½"
Setting triangles		
medium blue	16 E	eight squares 9⅞" x 9⅞" cut in half diagonally
	4 F	two squares 13⅝" x 13⅝" cut in half diagonally
Borders		
stripe	5 inner border strips	1¼" x 40"
print	6 outer border strips	2" x 40"
Backing	2 panels	28" x 54"
Batting	1 panel	54" x 54"
Binding	6 strips	2½" x 40"

Fig. 1. Quilt assembly

border unit

Fig. 2. Border unit

"These curves are somewhat difficult to sew smoothly at first, especially piecing A-2 to A-3. Take your time pinning and easing the pieces together, and stitch slowly. Adjust the fabric every ½" or so as you sew. Luckily, the arcs are very short, and they go quickly once you get the feel of them." Janet

3. Look at the quilt photo and arrange the diamond blocks accordingly. Sew two E triangles to each block-1 diamond to make eight wedge-shaped units (fig. 1).

4. Use set-in seams to add a block-2 diamond to each wedge unit. Join the wedge units in pairs then join the pairs. Add the F triangles to the corners of the quilt.

5. Sew the inner border strips together, end to end with diagonal seams, to make one continuous strip. Cut four 48" strips from the continuous strip.

6. In the same way, sew the outer border strips together and cut four 51" strips from the continuous strip.

7. Matching their centers, sew an inner border strip to each outer border strip to make a border unit (fig. 2).

8. Sew a border unit to each side of the quilt and miter the corners, matching the seam lines where the inner and outer borders join. Trim off any extra border length, leaving a ¼" seam allowance.

9. Layer the quilt top, batting, and backing; baste. Quilt the layers. (Refer to our suggested quilting ideas on page 18 if you need inspiration.) Then bind the raw edges to complete your quilt.

Using Gradient Colors

A sensible way to handle piecing spikes in gradient colors, and keep them in order, is to paper piece the arcs in a production-line style. For example, stack up all eight section B paper patterns and sew the first two fabrics on all of them. Then, sew the next fabric to all eight arc sections. This method really helps maintain the correct color sequence because, if you only have one stack of fabric in front of you, you can't pick up a wrong color.

CRESSIDA

CRESSIDA, by Deb Karasik and Janet Mednick

Quilt size 82¾" x 82¾"
Diamond blocks finish 10" on a side

After playing awhile with the diamond block we had designed for SPIKE REDUX (page 56), we decided to go further and see what would happen. We dropped a second arc into the block and arranged these new, more complex diamonds into various settings. When we tried a Lone Star setting, fabulous things happened. One of them was this quilt.

It was quite a "eureka" moment when we stumbled across a yellow-orange ombre fabric in a shop. With one look at each other, we knew right away we needed it and how we'd use it. See the center star area? See how it's darker orange in the middle, fades to yellow between the arcs, and returns to orange at the tips? That is a single piece of fabric.

Note: The measurements for precutting spike and background fabrics are based on the dimensions of the largest pieces. If you would rather conserve fabric for the diamond blocks, see Precutting Fabrics on page 13.

Triangle block
colorway-1, make 16
colorway-2, make 48

Yardage	
Use fabric at least 40" wide.	
Fabrics	**Yards**
Aqua	3⅝
Aqua to dark teal scraps	4¾
Golden yellow	2⅛
Purple-1	6⅛
Purple-2	½
Red	1⅝
Red orange	6⅝
Yellow-orange gradation	2
Backing	8
Binding	¾

See cutting chart on page 68.

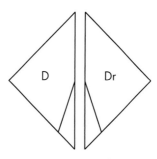

Setting triangles
colorway-1, make 8 each
colorway-2, make 8 each

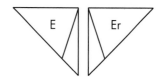

Setting triangles
make 8 each

Border block, make 20

Cutting
Cut strips selvage to selvage.

Fabrics	Pieces	Cut
Center star		
purple-1	16 A	2½" x 6¼"
aqua to dark teal scraps	160 B spikes	1" x 5¾"
	8 D-1	8½" x 11"
	8 Dr-1	8½" x 11"
golden yellow	176 B backgrounds	2½" x 6"
yellow-orange gradation	16 C	2" x 20"
purple-2	8 D-2	3" x 8"
	8 Dr-2	3" x 8"
Outer ring		
purple-1	32 A	2½" x 6¼"
aqua to dark teal scraps	480 B spikes	1" x 5¾"
red	16 A	2½" x 6¼"
red-orange	528 B backgrounds	2¼" x 6"
	8 D-2	3" x 8"
	8 Dr-2	3" x 8"
	8 E-2	4½" x 5½"
	8 Er-2	4½" x 5½"
yellow-orange gradation	48 C	2" x 20"
aqua	8 D-1	8½" x 11"
	8 Dr-1	8½" x 11"
	8 E-1	5" x 10½"
	8 Er-1	5" x 10½"
	4 F	10½" x 10½"
Inner border		
aqua	8 strips	2½" x 40"
Outer border		
red	20 A	2½" x 6"
	100 B spikes	1¾" x 6"
	4 H	6½" x 6½"
purple-1	120 B backgrounds	3" x 6"
	20 C	4½" x 16"
	40 G	4" x 8¼"
	40 Gr	4" x 8¼"
Backing	3 panels	32" x 91"
Batting	1 panel	91" x91"
Binding	9 strips	2½" x 40"

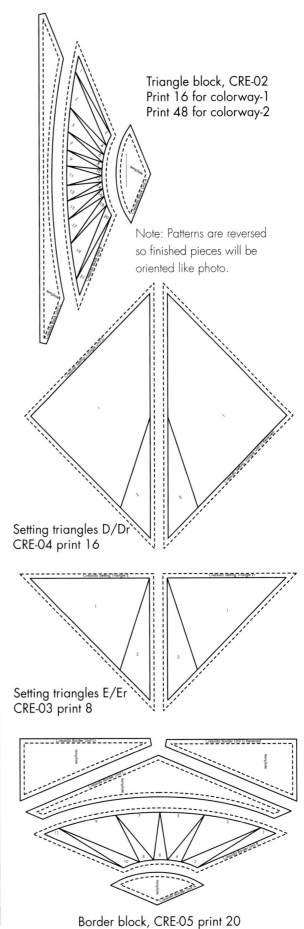

Triangle block, CRE-02
Print 16 for colorway-1
Print 48 for colorway-2

Note: Patterns are reversed so finished pieces will be oriented like photo.

Setting triangles D/Dr CRE-04 print 16

Setting triangles E/Er CRE-03 print 8

Border block, CRE-05 print 20

Assembly

1. Print 64 triangle block foundations and 20 border block foundations from the CD. As they are needed, cut the fabric pieces listed in the cutting table.

2. Referring to Sewing Spikes (page 14) and Sewing Arcs (page 16), make the blocks shown in the block diagrams. Remove the paper foundations.

3. Print the following triangle foundations from the CD: sixteen D, sixteen Dr, eight E, and eight Er. Make the setting triangles as shown in figure 1. *Do not sew the triangle pairs together. Instead, sew the setting triangles to the spiky triangle blocks.*

4. Join the triangles to the center star and outer ring blocks as shown in figure 2. Repeat to make four quadrants.

5. Add the F corner squares to each quadrant with set-in seams, then sew the quadrants together.

6. Sew the inner border strips together, end to end with diagonal seams, to make one continuous strip. Using your quilt's measurements, cut two side border strips from the continuous strip. Sew them to the quilt. Repeat for the top and bottom borders.

7. Print 20 border diamond block foundations from the CD. Make the blocks shown in the block diagrams. Add the G and Gr triangles to complete the blocks then remove the paper foundations. Join the blocks to make four border strips, as shown in figure 3, page 70.

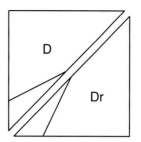

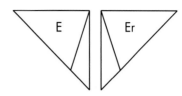

Fig. 1. Setting triangles

Fig. 2. Quadrant assembly

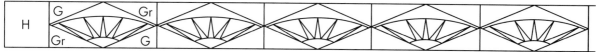

Fig. 3. Border strip

8. Sew two of the strips to the sides of the quilt. Add the H squares to the ends of the remaining border strips and sew them to the top and bottom to complete the quilt top.

9. Layer the quilt top, batting, and backing; baste. Quilt the layers, referring to our suggested quilting ideas on page 18 if you need inspiration. Then bind the raw edges to complete your quilt.

"We can't find any more of the ombre fabric, and we've looked, so you probably won't be able to either. This being the case, you won't be able to exactly recreate CRESSIDA. *That's OK, though. As we've probably said before, we truly believe quilters should make quilts their own by choosing alternate fabrics and colors that please them. Might we suggest a mottled batik in its place? You won't be able to fussy cut exact duplicates for each piece, but allowing the batik colors to fall where they may will definitely help your version glow in its very own way!" Deb & Janet*

Quilt assembly

ILLUMINATA

ILLUMINATA, by Deb Karasik and Janet Mednick

Quilt size 72" x 72"

Blocks 11" x 11" finished

When folks see ILLUMINATA for the first time, the reaction is always the same. "Wow, do you think those are all separate pieces?" Of course, the answer is yes!

Although there is only one basic block in this quilt, the spikes in each section are cut from a gradient run of colors, and so are the backgrounds. We also had to maintain the contrast. This is one of the most intense quilts we have done. So, if ILLUMINATA is your choice to make, take a deep breath and start cutting strips.

Yardage Use fabric at least 40" wide.	
Fabrics	**Yards**
Black	6¼
Color runs	scraps
Multicolor print	⅞
Backing	4¾
Binding	⅝

See cutting chart on page 74.

Note: Using the authors' method of cutting all the spike and background pieces the same size will require a lot more fabric. You can conserve fabric (see Precutting Fabrics on page 13), but that may limit your flexibility when it comes to arranging the colors in the blocks.

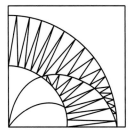

Main block, make 24

Border block 1, make 24

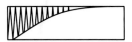

Border block 2, make 4

Border block 3, make 4

Border corner, make 4

Assembly

1. Print the block foundations from the CD. You will need a foundation for each block. As they are needed, cut the fabrics listed in the cutting table, page 74.

2. Referring to Sewing Spikes (page 14) and Sewing Arcs (page 16), make all the blocks as shown in the diagrams. Remove the paper foundations.

Cutting		
Cut strips selvage to selvage.		
Fabrics	**Pieces**	**Cut**
Main block		
black	24 A-1	4½" x 7"
	24 A-3	3½" x 7"
	24 D	11½" x 11½"
color run 1	192 B spikes	2" x 6"
color run 2	216 B backgrounds	2" x 6"
color run 3	360 C spikes	2" x 6"
color run 4	384 C backgrounds	2" x 6"
multicolor print	24 A-2	4½" x 6½"
Border block 1		
color run 1	288 spikes	1½" x 4"
color run 2	312 backgrounds	1½" x 4"
Border blocks 2 & 3		
black	8 A	4" x 11½"
color run 1	96 B spikes	1½" x 4"
color run 2	104 B backgrounds	1½" x 4"
Border corner		
color run 1	32 A spikes	1½" x 4"
color run 2	38 A backgrounds	1½" x 4"
color run 3	60 B spikes	1½" x 4"
color run 4	64 B backgrounds	1½" x 4"
Plain block		
black	12 squares	11½" x 11½"
Backing	2 panels	40" x 80"
Batting	1 panel	80" x 80"
Binding	8 strips	2½" x 40"

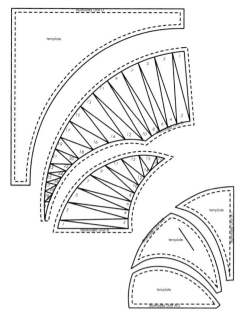

Main block, ILL-02, print 24

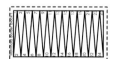

Border block 1, ILL-06, print 24

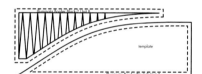

Border block 2, ILL-4, print 4

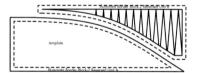

Border block 3, ILL-05, print 4

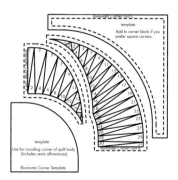

Corner, ILL-03, print 4

Note: Patterns are reversed so finished pieces will be oriented like photo.

3. Square up your blocks, if necessary. The main blocks should be 11½" x 11½", which includes seam allowances. Border block 1 needs to be 3½" x 6½". Blocks 2 and 3 are 3½" x 11½". See figure 1 for the border corner measurements.

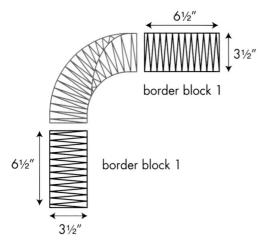

Fig. 1. Border corner (Measurements include seam allowances.)

4. Look at the quilt photo and arrange the main blocks accordingly. Sew the blocks together in rows then join the rows.

5. Print 24 border block 1 and 4 each of border block 2, 3, and the corner border blocks. Make the border blocks and arrange them as shown in figure 2 to make a border strip. Make four strips.

Color Strategy

We used the same-sized precut fabric strips for the spikes and backgrounds of all the main blocks. Why? Because the strips could then be used in all areas, large or small, of any main block. So we used about a zillion (over 1,200 actually) 2" x 6" strips. Not to worry. They weren't all different. We use the same fabrics over and over. We laid out four to five sets of color gradations, each with eight to ten strips, with contrast between the rows. You get the idea.

Gradations can really make your quilt sing if you're willing to put the time into arranging them. It's not really necessary to continue a color gradation into the next block. When you lay out the color runs on your work table, you will probably rearrange them a hundred times. We did! Seriously though, concentrate on one arc at a time.

"It's easiest if you work color by color. We started with our yellows, moved on to the greens, then the blues. Then, we started combining colors, purple blended to greens, red blended into yellow . . . and so on."

three of border block 1   border block 2   border block 3   three of border block 1

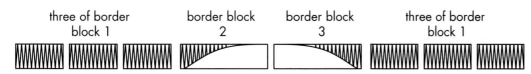

Fig. 2. Border strip

Sewing Strategy

We sewed all of the B and C units before assembling any blocks. Why? We found that some gradation combinations looked better than others. By piecing all of the B and C units before moving on, you will be able to play with them on a design wall until you get the arc combinations that really please you.

The trick in sewing the B and C units together is removing the paper from unit B, but leaving it on unit C. Be careful not to stretch the B unit out of shape. Pin the beginning and the end of the arc seam and gently ease unit B onto unit C.

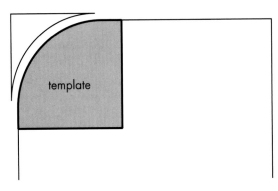

Fig. 3. Cutting corners

6. Use the border corner template to make a template from lightweight cardboard or template plastic. The template includes seam allowances.

7. Use the template to mark the curved corners on the quilt body. Cut the curves (fig. 3).

8. Sew a border strip to each of the four sides of the quilt. Sew the border corners to the quilt with set-in seams.

9. Layer the quilt top, batting, and backing; baste. Quilt the layers. (Refer to our suggested quilting ideas on page 18 if you need inspiration.)

10. Cut bias strips from the binding fabric square. Sew the strips together, end to end, to make one continuous binding strip approximately 300" long. Use this strip to bind the quilt's raw edges.

11. Layer the quilt top, batting, and backing; baste. Quilt the layers. (Refer to our suggested quilting ideas on page 18 if you need inspiration.) Then bind the raw edges to complete your quilt.

Quilting Illuminata

Now you have your top done, staring at you from your design wall. How in the world should a quilt of this magnitude be quilted? We toyed with quite a few quilting motifs, some standard, some really far out. As you can see from the close-ups, less is more. There is already so much going on in this quilt, over-quilting it would only add visual confusion.

We chose simple, but complementary designs and threads that finished this quilt off nicely. Beautiful threads, even applied sparingly, will add those breathtaking touches that everyone will notice. The exotic threads, such as the huge variety of metallics, are definitely worth learning how to use. Experiment with tension and needle size when you use these threads.

Quilt assembly

chapter 6

Outside the Box

W e did LILY IN DISGUISE simultaneoulsy with CRESSIDA (page 66) as a sort of break from working on skewed blocks. All of the blocks together gave the appearance of water, so we chose a border that resembles a gentle stream flowing around the quilt. It was simple piecing, and the effect really worked with the blocks. The project went together in just a couple of weeks, including the quilting. Yes, we are total manics, but sometimes the quilts just possses us.

LILY IN DISGUISE
Bonus Blocks

LILY IN DISGUISE, by Deb Karasik and Janet Mednick

This quilt shows how you can create just about anything if you play with blocks and placement. For your project, we give you five blocks to get you started. And instead of telling you how many of each block you need, we suggest you sew a few of them and see how they look with each other on your design wall. That way, you will be able to see what needs to be filled in. As the quilt starts to come together, it will take on a life of its own.

"LILY IN DISGUISE was the first quilt Janet and I worked on together that I quilted. It was a real leap of faith on Janet's part to entrust me with quilting this all on my own. I was a true novice. I had only quilted one small wallhanging before this. So, once again I will stress, if I can do it, you can do it." Deb

"It wasn't a leap of any sort for me. I knew Deb's quilting would do it justice. I assumed I'd get a turn at quilting, too, but Deb maniacally quilted it to completion. All I could say was "Wow, great job!" Janet

Bonus Blocks

Border block LIL-02

Border block LIL-03

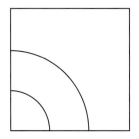

Border corner block LIL-01

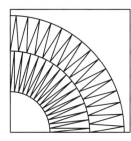

Block LIL-04

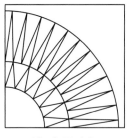

Block LIL-05

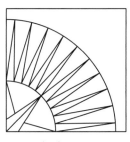

Block LIL-06

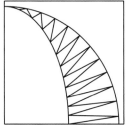

Block LIL-07

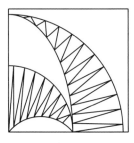

Block LIL-08

NAPA VALLEY AT SUNSET (80" x 80"), by Deb Karasik. Being comfortable with bright, jewel tone fabrics, I purposely chose colors I wasn't comfortable with. Then I designed a quilt that also challenged my piecing experience.

SPIKE'S REVENGE (74" x 74"), by Deb Karasik and Janet Mednick. When I designed this quilt, it didn't have a spiky border … but somehow, one magically appeared. Janet quilted it for me as a gift.

COTTON CANDY TWIST (44" x 44"), by Betty Tang, San Francisco, California. This quilt is based on the RASPBERRY PARFAIT class I took with Deb.

CUBIST ORBS, ABOVE, (36" x 56"), by Janet Mednick. During a guild retreat, I took a class with Cara Gulati and "had to" add spikes to her pattern RADIANT SUNS.

SERENDIPITOUS LEAVES, LEFT, (30" x 36"), Janet Mednick. I designed and made this quilt during a four-day class with Caryl Bryer Fallert at Art Quilt Tahoe. Taking classes from the masters keeps us growing.

FAR FLUNG FIONA (68" x 88"), by Deb Karasik. At a quilt retreat that Janet and I hosted, we took a class with Cara Gulati. Although her pattern RADIANT SUNS had no spikes, I just couldn't resist putting them in mine.

SPIKE MANIA (54" x 54"), by Sue Deal, Petaluma, California. This quilt is also from a class I took with Deb. It is based on WHIRLIGIG (page 47).

COTTON CANDY CLASS (44" x 44"), by Trudy Gee, San Francisco, California. This was a quilt I made in a class with Deb. It is based on the RASPBERRY SORBET quilt (page 51).

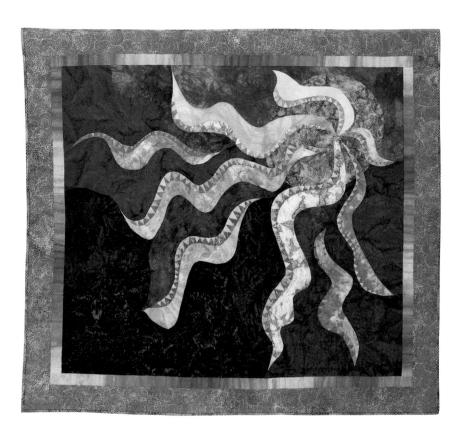

MOON IN RETROGRADE, ABOVE, (54" x 38"), by Deb Karasik. After completing a class with Caryl Bryer Fallert at Art Quilt Tahoe, I decided to try the technique again and came up with this quilt.

IN THE BLINK OF AN EYE, LEFT, (32" x 40"), by Deb Karasik. This quilt was made in a class with Caryl Bryer Fallert, but I felt it just "had to" have spikes, don't you think?

AARON'S QUILT (40" x 40"), by Deb Karasik. I designed this quilt for my grandson Aaron. He takes great delight in pointing out all the bugs and worms that are in the sashings.

TEQUILA SUNRISE (48" x 48"), by Sue Deal, Petaluma, California. This quilt was from a class I took with Deb. It gave me a chance to use all my wonderful batiks.

AUTUMN CALLS (44" x 44"), by Deb Karasik. Made as a class sample for the first spiky class I ever taught. (See ROLLING SPIRALS pattern, page 31.)

JUNGLE JU JU (47" x 47"), by Janet Mednick. This QuiltMaven design continues to push the envelope with more spikes, more arcs, and more difficult piecing. Color choices were made as the stitching progressed.

Meet the Authors

DEB KARASIK

Deb dabbled in quilting when her children were born BRC (Before Rotary Cutters). But then she put down her scissors and cardboard templates and took up the task of raising her children and launching a career in the interior design industry. Her youngest daughter's announcement in 2000 that she was pregnant with triplets was all the incentive Deb needed to try quilting once again.

She ventured off to her local quilt shop and was introduced to the rotary cutter. With the discovery of this amazing tool, and all the luscious fabrics that were available for quilters, her new passion was born.

In these few short years of working in and honing this art form, Deb has designed and made numerous original quilts. Despite the fact (or perhaps because) she had no official art training or background, she had no preconceived boundaries as to design or color choices. When you view her quilts, this freedom of design and joyful use of color is instantly apparent.

In 2001 she met Janet Mednick at the San Francisco Quilter's Guild, and they became not only fast friends but also collaborators on many quilt projects.

JANET MEDNICK

Janet was born and raised in the Bronx, New York, and learned all types of needlework from her mother. She dabbled in paints and pencils as well, but her college education included few art courses. She and her husband, Avram, an educator and writer, relocated to San Francisco in the early '80s, where they raised their son Matthew and where Janet has been employed in the music merchandising business for twenty years. For more than fifteen years, she has been designing and making quilts in the evenings and on weekends, and she has won numerous ribbons at local quilt shows. She and Deb both enjoy the fun and camaraderie of team projects. Together and separately, they continue to design and create quilts (still in the evening and on weekends) that visually push the limits of the usual concept of "quilt."

Other AQS Books

This is only a small selection of the books available from the American Quilter's Society. AQS books are known worldwide for timely topics, clear writing, beautiful color photos, and accurate illustrations and patterns. The following books are available from your local bookseller, quilt shop, or public library.

#7073 us$24.95

#6905 us$24.95

#6902 us$22.95

#6681 us$24.95

#7042 us$29.95

#4545 us$18.95

#6514 us$21.95

#6899 us$21.95

#6677 us$21.95

Look for these books nationally.
Call or *Visit* our Web site at

1-800-626-5420
www.AmericanQuilter.com